THE CONSTRUCTION

AND

REARTICULATION OF RACE

IN A POST-RACIAL AMERICA

BY

Christopher J. Metzler

aberdeen university
press services

Printed in the United States of America
ISBN: 978-0-6152-1670-6

This book is printed on 6" x 9", perfect binding, 60# cream interior paper, black and white interior ink, 100# white exterior paper, full-color exterior ink. Prices are subject to change.

THE CONSTRUCTION AND REARTICULATION OF RACE IN A POST-RACIAL
AMERICA
First Edition
Christopher J. Metzler

ACKNOWLEDGEMENTS

I begin by thanking my family for supporting me throughout this project. While they may not always agree with my views or analysis, they encouraged my work. This unwavering support made me stronger and will help me to deal with the venom that will no doubt be forthcoming after this edition is read, analyzed, and vilified. I also must thank Professors Crenshaw and Gregory at Columbia University in New York City. As a graduate student at Columbia, their groundbreaking work convinced me of the need to think about, analyze, and criticize issues of race in a highly contextualized way. Professor Crenshaw is an icon of the critical race studies movement and a highly personable and inspirational person. Professor Gregory provided opportunities for critical reflection on race while allowing me to make my own decisions.

My students at CUNY guided my thinking and made invaluable contributions as I crafted and recrafted the essays in this edition. My students at Cornell, particularly those who enrolled in my "Training Difficult Issues in Diversity" course, made clear that race, racism, oppression, and privilege are as relevant now as they were in the Jim Crow and pre-civil rights era. I must also thank my colleagues at the Oxford Roundtable in Oxford England who responded critically but thoughtfully to my presentation at Oxford, upon which these essays are based.

Finally, I dedicate this edition to my father, Kenneth Stephen Metzler, Sr., who has provided the guidance, compassion, and forgiveness that I have needed throughout my life. While we have not always agreed on how to approach subjects, he provided me with the tools to think clearly. It is his attention to my education at an early age that has served me so well. I also must pay homage to my maternal grandmother, Monica Charles, who ensured that at the age of two I could read, write, and reason. Her enduring dedication to me, and my success, is humbling. To my mother, Ingrid Metzler, the rock of my very existence and my biggest and most ardent supporter and critic, I say thank you.

CONTENTS

Acknowledgements   i

Forward   v

IN THE BEGINNING THERE WAS SLAVERY   1

HUMAN RIGHTS: ANATOMY OF ABANDONMENT   9

THE PERFECT STORM: POLITICS, RACE, AND ECONOMICS   18

COMMUNISM, RACE-BAITING, AND BACK-BITING   24

HE AIN'T WHITE, HE'S MY BROTHER   36

YEZ UM MS. ROOSEVELT   39

THE RED BADGE OF SHAME   48

OF EGOS, INFIGHTING, AND THE NAACP   56
    The UDHR and Its Individualistic Underpinnings   66
    Collective Rights   69

THE AMERICAN CONSTRUCTION OF
HETERONORMATIVE MASCULINITY   73
    Performing Masculinity: Black, Red, Brown, and
    White All Over   77
    Exporting Hegemonic Masculinity: Actions,
    Reactions, and Consequences   79
    Masculinity, Patriarchy, and Relationship   82

Black Masculinity and the Civil Rights Movement   83
The Rap on Reparations   94

RACE IS A STATE OF MIND   98
Bootstrapping, Victimology, and Colorblindness:
The Neoconservative View   101
Cement Boot Straps and Decontextualization:
A Critique of the Neoconservative View   104
The Class Theorists: It's The Class Line,
Not The Color Line   107
Critique of the Class Theory   108
View From the Neo-Left   110
Critique Of The Neo-Left View   111
Self-Defining Identity Politics and the
Promise of Equality   113

ADDING SOME CONTEXT   116
Film and Law   120

TELEVISION   123
Mississippi Burning   123
Ole' Mis'   124
The Articulation of Race   126

FILM AS A LEGAL LENS   129

**EMANCIPATION, RECONSTRUCTION,
AND MISREPRESENTATION**   135

THE CIVIL RIGHTS MOVEMENT AND THE BLACK MAN   140

ENVISIONING THE REPRESENTATIONAL BLACK MAN   147

Afterward   151

Bibliography   163

FOREWORD

It is not controversial to say that America has had a conflicted and shameful history with race and racism. This history has included constructing race to justify slavery, legalized racism, and pretending that racism does not exist. Given that we live in a racialized society, why is it so hard to have a meaningful and substantive discussion about race? What roles do individual racists play? Who benefits from keeping the racial conversation alive? Has America exported its construction of race such that its racist images and stereotypes of blacks have been taken up by the rest of the world? What role has the NAACP played in the abandonment of human rights that has allowed race to continue to be an issue in America today? What is a "post-racial" America? How does one transcend race in a racist society? Why is the media afraid of race? What role does internalized oppression play in race? Is Derrick Bell correct when he writes that "racial equality is, in fact, not a realistic goal. By constantly aiming for a status that is unobtainable in a perilously racist America, black Americans face frustration and despair. Over time, our persistent quest for integration has hardened into self-defeating rigidity."[1]

Members of the American media have moved from reporting the news to advancing their opinions and discussing race in a roundabout

---

[1] Derrick Bell, "Racial Realism," *Connecticut Law Review* 24.2 (1992): 363.

way, which they claim is race neutral,[2] but which is in fact race conscious.[3] How has their unfettered power defined the coverage of Barack Obama and Hillary Clinton in the 2008 Democratic primary? What role does rap music, with its revival of the most vile and base stereotypes of black men from slavery and the Jim Crow era and its attendant culture of debauchery, play in stoking racial subordination and domination? Does the fact that so many rap artists are black provide them with the veritable black pass to lyrically and virtually debase and defile black women and themselves that whites, by virtue of their whiteness, are denied?

This book attempts to put race and a racial America into context, so people can begin to have a discussion about race that is meaningful and substantive. This is a first edition, and as such is intended to start the conversation. Where the conversation leads depends largely upon how intentional and robust a conversation people are willing to have about the continuing significance of race in America, as well as what, if any actions they are willing to take upon the conversation's conclusion. It also depends on how honestly people are willing to view the historical and critical approach to race that I present in this book. It is not my intention to tell people what to think about race, what to do about race, or how to respond to race; I leave that to the individual. My hope is that

---

[2] By race neutral, I mean that the majority of those in the media want us to believe that their reporting on race is neutral, impersonal, and somehow developed without regard to their own socialization and or experiences with race or lack thereof.

[3] The reality is that the vast majority of those in the American media who construct, analyze, and report on race are predominantly white. With the advent and proliferation of 24-hour cable television, the Internet, and the "shame shows" in which self-proclaimed media experts analyze social and political issues, including race, in an often cacophonous and churlish gabfest, has come a media discourse on race designed to dissuade consumers from forming their own opinions; instead, advocating for the jabbering sect's view of race. The jabbering sect's advocacy journalism promotes their particular racial pedigree, whether they wish to admit it or not. The same is true of the vast majority of black advocacy journalists. The fact that the black advocacy journalists are the numerical minority does not exempt them from race-conscious reporting. In fact, some people expect their reporting to be "authentically black." And on that score, they do not disappoint.

this book will serve as a guide to readers as they walk through the contested space of race. Readers may choose to simply ignore my thoughts, to blame their racial insecurities on me, or to engage my thoughts while disagreeing with my approach. In any event, I hope that this book furthers the debate and discussion on race in America that has become bogged down in ideology, political musings, and anemic approaches that defy solutions.

CHAPTER ONE
IN THE BEGINNING THERE WAS SLAVERY

Slavery and its lingering effects are situated at the core of why blacks are a largely marginalized and disenfranchised group and why many immigrant groups that have come to America post-slavery have prospered economically, and in some cases socially, beyond the levels experienced by blacks whose ancestors lived in America during slavery. However, to blame slavery and its lingering effects alone would be too simplistic and uncritical. We must instead interrogate internalized oppression, the role of the National Association for the Advancement of Colored People (NAACP), the role of globalization, as well as the cultural tools of film and formal equality to determine the role each has played and continues to play in the continuing significance of race in a post-slavery society.

As a legal matter, slavery was outlawed many years ago; however its social and institutional effects continue to have a damaging impact on American society as a whole. An analysis of slavery in America reveals a path filled with turmoil, angst, and bitterly earned victories in the area of civil rights for blacks nationwide. The American government and all of its branches, especially the judiciary, were complicit in ensuring that gratuitous acts of violence and subordination were the rule rather than the exception.[4] As a general matter, lynchings, beatings, the refusal of voting privileges, the provision of substandard edu-

---

[4] See generally, Dred Scott v. Sandford, 60 U.S. 393, 1857; Plessey v. Ferguson, 163 U.S. 537, 1896; and The Slaughter House Cases, 83 U.S. 36, 1873.

cation, and the denial of privileges and immunities granted whites were all openly, notoriously, and shamelessly sanctioned by the United States Government. While the decision to abolish and outlaw slavery was one of the most important events in the nation's history, it was incomplete and impotent. That is, simply abolishing slavery was not enough to eradicate widely accepted sociological, psychological, and political theories of black inferiority. This is because America was built on exploitation, and fueled by racist, separatist thinking and ideology. Moreover, the proclamation of emancipation failed, as a practical matter to address how America would atone for its systematic and systemic practice of racial discrimination against blacks without shame, remorse, or apology.

Once the slaves were freed, attention turned toward identifying what the government and society had the intestinal fortitude to do to address the effects of slavery and discrimination. The answer, not surprisingly, was a resounding, "Not much." The solution offered was what Professors Crenshaw and Peller refer to as formal equality.

> This very struggle over meaning is precisely what the intense contestations about race in the law are really about. Rather than providing some kind of firm ground to challenge racist institutional practices, notions of formal equality, objectivity, neutrality, and the like tend to obscure the way that race is experienced by the vast majority of African-Americans in this society.[5]

Even when blacks were "given" the right to vote, the vote of a black man counted as only two-thirds of a vote according to the law. The law required blacks to sit at the backs of buses, eat in black restaurants, use restrooms and substandard water fountains designated for their use, and send their children to schools set aside for blacks that were by definition inferior in that they lacked the funding, materials, and physical facilities conducive to learning. The issue was not that the schools were black; it was that they were inferior.

As America continued to evolve, blacks individually and collectively worked to gain education and freedom—an endless uphill battle. While it was the job of the government to protect all Americans, it was

---

[5] Kimberle Crenshaw and Gary Peller, "The Contradictions of Mainstream Constitutional Theory," *UCLA L. Rev.* 45 (1998): 1683.

clear the government chose to protect only whites. Lynchings were not uncommon, especially in the South, and arrests for offenses such as drinking from the wrong fountain in the park were routinely sanctioned by the government and law enforcement agencies.

The establishment of the NAACP provided great hope to those who had suffered years of oppression and mistreatment at the hands of society and the government. The impetus, at least in part, for the forming of the NAACP was to respond to the flagrant and routine violations of the rights of blacks. The NAACP began as an organization concerned with securing civil and human rights for blacks. It was also initially concerned with exposing gross human rights violations. Blacks and whites in the newly formed NAACP and other organizations led the charge against discrimination and segregation in the United States.[6]

At first, the NAACP worked in all areas that had the potential to improve black life. The NAACP filed litigation against the government when blacks wanted to become soldiers and were initially refused entry. It filed again when black soldiers were given menial tasks while their white counterparts were provided training in areas that were more likely to lead to their gainful employment and would therefore improve their economic conditions. The NAACP led the charge against lynchings and devised the legal strategy in *Brown v. Board of Education* and its progeny. The NAACP was convinced that the lives of blacks would be improved through the use of a legalistic strategy steeped in civil rights.

The NAACP must be praised for its legal victories in securing civil rights for blacks. However, it must also be taken to task for its critical and fatal mistake of focusing on civil rights over human rights. Lynching was the most prolific human rights violation besetting blacks of that period. It was the human rights issue of the time and the NAACP failed to proactively and effectively use lynching as the catalyst that would have catapulted systemic discrimination against blacks into the ultimate civil rights issue. This is not to suggest that the failure is entirely the organization's fault; it is to suggest that given the organization's charge, it must bear responsibility for having moved its focus away

---

[6] *African American Odyssey: A Quest for Full Citizenship*, 21 Mar. 2008, The Library of Congress On-line Exhibition, 10 May 2008 <lcweb2.loc.gov/ammem/aaohtml/exhibit/aopart7.html>.

from human rights, thereby allowing formal equality to be accepted as the answer to the vexing question of racism.

The Jim Crow laws were a rallying point for the NAACP. Jim Crow was a character developed in 1830 that eventually provided the tag line for a set of laws that prohibited blacks from sitting at the front of a bus, going to certain public schools, and being allowed rights that others were born into.[7] Jim Crow has been said to have originated when a white minstrel show performer, Thomas "Daddy" Rice, blackened his face with charcoal paste or burnt cork and performed a silly jig while singing the lyrics to the song "Jump Jim Crow." Rice is said to have created the character while traveling in the South after having seen a crippled elderly black man (some say a young black boy) dancing and singing a song ending with the chorus words: "Weel about and turn about and do jis so, eb'ry time I weel about I jump Jim Crow."[8] Some historians have theorized that Mr. Crow owned the slave upon whom Rice based the character, thus the reference to Jim Crow in the lyrics.[9]

On the eve of the Civil War, the Jim Crow pejorative, along with that of Sambos, Coons, and Zip Dandies, had been indelibly etched into the minds of Americans and thus became a part of the cultural ethos. These denigrating terms encouraged whites to view blacks as subhuman buffoons, unworthy of respect, value, or human rights.

> The public symbols and constant reminders of his inferior positions were the segregation statutes, or 'Jim Crow' laws. They constituted the most elaborate and formal expression of sovereign white opinion upon the subject. In bulk and in detail as well as in effectiveness of enforcement the segregation codes were comparable with the black codes of the old regime, though the laxity that mitigated the harshness of the black codes was replaced by a rigidity that was more typical of the segregation code. That code led the sanction of law to a racial

---

[7] Ronald L. F. Davis, "Creating Jim Crow: In-Depth Essay," *The History of Jim Crow*, New York Life, 10 May 2008 <http://www.jimcrow history.org/history/creating2.htm>.

[8] C. V. Woodward, *The Strange Career of Jim Crow*, 3rd rev. ed. (New York: Oxford University Press, 1974) 7.

[9] Woodward 7.

ostracism that extended to churches and schools, to housing and jobs, to eating and drinking.[10]

The Jim Crow era in America began in 1890 when southern states adopted a system that strengthened laws and state provisions designed to further reduce the societal and legal position of blacks to one that was to be permanently subordinate to the white man. The laws were designed for the purpose of separating the races in public places including parks, schools, transportation, and eating establishments.

Segregation and disfranchisement laws were often supported, moreover, by brutal acts of ceremonial and ritualized mob violence (lynchings) against southern blacks. Indeed, from 1889 to 1930, over 3,700 men and women were reported lynched in the United States—most were southern blacks. Hundreds of other lynchings and acts of mob terror aimed at brutalizing blacks occurred throughout the era but went unreported in the press.[11]

The Supreme Court of the United States was a willing accomplice in the construction of white maleness dripping with hegemony. In 1883, the Supreme Court ruled unconstitutional the Civil Rights Act of 1875. The statute read in relevant part that "all persons [...] (emphasis supplied) shall be entitled to full and equal enjoyment of the accommodations, facilities, and privileges of inns, public conveyances on land or water, theaters and other places of public amusements."[12] Among the public sites included in the cases reviewed by the court involving acts of discrimination were a railroad, a theater in San Francisco, and the Grand Opera House in New York. Chief Justice Bradley, writing for the majority, declared the federal law unconstitutional holding that the Fourteenth Amendment did not protect black people from discrimination by private entities and individuals; such discrimination he said could not be practiced by the states. The chief justice went on to say that it "was time for blacks to assume the rank of mere citizen (empha-

[10] Woodward 7.

[11] Davis par. 4.

[12] Civil Rights Act of 1875, 18 Stat. 335 (1875), Section 1.

sis supplied) and stop being the special favorite of these laws."[13] Embolden by this decision, southern states began a campaign to continue to segregate and thus continue to construct black male imagery. In 1890, Louisiana enacted a law requiring that blacks ride in separate railroad cars. The law was subsequently challenged by Homére Plessey, a light-skinned black man who boarded a train and sat in the section reserved for whites. He was, of course, arrested and both the trial court and the United States Supreme Court ruled against him. The court, in the infamous *Plessey v. Ferguson* case ruled that Plessey's rights were not denied him because the separate accommodations provided to blacks were equal to whites. It also ruled that "separate but equal" accommodations did not stamp the "colored race with a badge of inferiority." As a result of *Plessey*, it became clear that the court constructed race. As Professor Lopez has observed:

> As a category, 'white' was constructed by prerequisite courts in a two-step process that ultimately defined not just the boundaries of the group, but its identity as well. First, the courts constructed the bounds of whiteness by deciding on a case-by-case basis who was *not* white. Though the prerequisite courts were charged with defining the term 'white person,' they did not do so by referring to a freestanding notion of whiteness. No court offered a complete typology listing the characteristics of whiteness against which to compare the petitioner. Instead, the courts defined 'white' through a process of negation, systematically identifying who was non-white.[14]

In 1875, the courts were asked to provide clarity as to which forms of discrimination were prohibited against blacks and which were allowed. As a jurisprudential matter, the courts ruled that the Constitution only prohibited discrimination against blacks by government bodies such as states; however, the judges ruled that businesses and private citizens could discriminate against blacks without implicating the United States Constitution. In the court's view, "state action," that is, acting with state law as a cover when engaging in discrimination, was a thre-

---

[13] Civil Rights Cases, 109 U.S. 3 (1883) (109).

[14] Ian F. Haney Lopez, *White By Law* (New York University Press, 1996), 27.

threshold act required before the Constitution could be violated. Absent state action, acts targeting blacks for discrimination because of their race were permissible and outside the realm of the courts' jurisdiction.

In 1890, when the federal government passed laws prohibiting similar discrimination, states began to enact their own laws exempting hotels, railroads, and other businesses, thereby effectively continuing to allow discrimination. Throughout, the black population continued to fight against basic human rights violations, including public lynchings. As these events were taking place, the NAACP scrambled to advocate for change on the human rights and civil rights issues that it could impact. Initially, the NAACP focused on both human and civil rights through the use of lawsuits and other legal measures.

As World War II drew to an end, the problems of segregation and inequality were still a reality of American society. Racism, both blatant and vitriolic, was still the rule and not the exception for blacks. In the context of American life, both the civil and human rights of blacks were routinely being violated; human rights being the rights belonging to a person simply because they are born human, and civil rights being those rights provided through laws and which can be taken away by legislators as easily as they are given. Professor Crenshaw puts the problem of civil rights in the American context best.

> Prior to civil rights, blacks were formally subordinated by the state. Blacks experienced being the "other" in two aspects of oppression which I shall designate as symbolic and material. Symbolic subordination refers to the formal denial of social and political equality to all blacks, regardless of their accomplishments. Segregation and other forms of social exclusion—separate restrooms, drinking fountains, entrances, parks, cemeteries, and dining facilities—reinforced a racist ideology that blacks were inferior to whites and were therefore not included in the vision of America as a community of equals.[15]

Although written in 1988, Professor Crenshaw's analysis exposes the fundamental contradictions of an ostensibly post-racial America. Simply put, "post-racial" is a moniker that represents an articulated vision

[15] K. W. Crenshaw, "Race Reform, Retrenchment: Transformation and Legitimization in Anti-Discrimination Law," *Harvard L. Rev.*, 101 (1988): 1377.

of race steeped in rigid ideology, constrained by denial of historical realities and undermined by a need to move forward without acknowledging racism, exclusion, and oppression as continuing violations that impact all Americans, including whites.

CHAPTER TWO
HUMAN RIGHTS: ANATOMY OF ABANDONMENT

Human rights are frequently held to be universal in the sense that all people have and should enjoy them, and to be independent in the sense that they exist and are available as standards of justification and criticism, whether or not they are recognized and implemented by the legal system or officials of a country.[16]

> Human rights law is an important component of a project of liberation because in its short formal existence it has effectively reconstituted omnipotent power of the state to do as it wished with its subjects wherever they might be and even with anyone who found himself or herself within its territorial jurisdiction. Human rights law is revolutionary from a stasis perspective in that it renders individual subjects, rather than just objects, in international law. [H]uman rights language then, is a morally compelling tool for denouncing sovereign actions that derogate the dignity of personhood and citizenship.[17]

---

[16] James W., Nickel, *Making Sense of Human Rights: Philosophical Reflections on the Universal Declaration of Human Rights* (Berkeley: University of California Press, 1987).

[17] Esperanza Berta Hernandez-Truyol, "Breaking Cycles of Inequality: Critical Theory, Human Rights, and Family Injustice," *Crossroads, Directions, and a New Critical Race Theory,* eds. Francisco Valdes, Jerome McCristal Culp, and Angela P. Harris (Philadelphia: Temple University Press, 2002) 346.

Human rights are commonly understood to be those rights inherent to all human beings. The concept of human rights acknowledges that every single human being is entitled to enjoy his or her human rights without distinction as to race, color, gender, language, religion, political or other opinion, national or social origin, property, birth, or other status. Human rights are legally guaranteed by human rights laws, which protect individuals and groups against actions that interfere with fundamental freedoms and human dignity. They are expressed in treaties, customary international laws, bodies of principles, and other sources of law. Human rights law places an obligation on states to act in a particular way and prohibits states from engaging in specified activities. However, the law does not establish human rights. Human rights are entitlements that are accorded to every person as a consequence of being human. Treaties and other sources of law generally serve to formally protect the rights of individuals and groups against actions or abandonment of actions by governments that interfere with the enjoyment of their human rights.

Human rights are broad in both scope and application. There is no requirement that they be bestowed on human beings by any entity. At their core is the universal concept of humanness. Persons respecting humanity do so because they are human, not because the law tells them to do so. The following are some of the most important characteristics of human rights:

- They are founded on respect for the dignity and worth of each person.
- They are universal, meaning that they are applied equally and without discrimination to all people.
- They are inalienable, in that no one can have his or her human rights taken away, except in specific situations. For example, the right to liberty can be restricted if a person is found guilty of a crime by a court of law.
- They are indivisible, interrelated, and interdependent, because it is insufficient to respect some human rights and not others.
- In practice, the violation of one right will often affect several other rights. All human rights should therefore be seen as hav-

ing equal importance and being equally essential to the dignity and worth of every person.[18]

The United Nations' (UN) first major achievement in the field of human rights was the General Assembly's adoption of the Universal Declaration of Human Rights in 1948. Members of the UN disputed the wording of the Universal Declaration at the time, but the declaration was finally adopted by consensus. The Universal Declaration is an eloquent and far-reaching description of the rights of all human beings. In addition, it gives individuals a place in international law they never had before. Many other human rights instruments are based on the Universal Declaration. Some of the fundamental rights cited in the Declaration are:

- the right to equality and freedom from discrimination;
- the right to life, liberty, and personal security;
- freedom from torture and degrading treatment;
- the right to equality before the law;
- the right to a fair trial;
- the right to privacy;
- freedom of belief and religion;
- freedom of opinion;
- freedom of peaceful assembly and association;
- the right to participate in government;
- the right to social security;
- the right to work;
- the right to an adequate standard of living; and
- the right to education.[19]

This book argues that the decision by the NAACP to put forth a very legalistic civil rights strategy instead of a broader human rights strategy is at least partly responsible for America's failure to pay its

---

[18] The *Universal Declaration of Human Rights* (1948) was drafted by the UN Commission on Human Rights in 1947 and 1948. The Declaration was adopted by the United Nations General Assembly on 10 Dec. 1948.

[19] Office of the United Nations High Commissioner for Human Rights (OHCHR), *Leaflet No.2: Indigenous Peoples, the UN and Human Rights*, 10 Jan. 2008 <http://www.ohchr.org/Documents/Publications/GuideIP leaflet2en.pdf> p. 5.

racial debt. In addition, the Cold War and the superficial and mistaken viewpoint that Eleanor Roosevelt was the "ultimate friend of the Negro" had devastating and long lasting effects on the construction, articulation, and exportation of race.

I now turn to the history of the NAACP and its fight for civil rights. This section briefly deconstructs the history and operations of the NAACP during its initial quest for human and then civil rights. The NAACP was conceived and born in Canada. It was there, in 1905, that a group of almost 30 black intellectuals gathered together to consider what type of aggressive action they could take to protect the freedom of blacks in America. As the first collective attempt by blacks to demand full citizenship rights in the 20th century, the Niagara Movement marks a major turning point in black history. The roots of the NAACP are founded in a race riot that occurred in 1908 in Springfield, Illinois. It was after gratuitous violence was perpetrated against blacks in the area that a group of liberal whites, including Mary White Ovington and Oswald Garrison Villard, called for a meeting to discuss racial justice. Of the 60 participants in attendance at that first meeting, six were black and included W. E. B. Du Bois. "Echoing the focus of Du Bois' militant all-black Niagara Movement, the NAACP's stated goal was to secure for all people the rights guaranteed in the 13th, 14th, and 15th Amendments to the United States Constitution, which promised an end to slavery, the equal protection of the law, and universal adult male suffrage, respectively."[20]

The first national office for the NAACP was established in New York City. The next step was to name a board of directors and a president. The first NAACP president was a white man named Moorfield Storey. At that time, only one black person was appointed to the board of directors. It was Du Bois and he was made director of publications because of his experience as a journalist. In 1910, Du Bois established the official journal of the organization and named it *The Crisis*. According to Du Bois:

> The object of this publication is to set forth those facts and arguments which show the danger of race prejudice, particularly

[20] NAACP, "Black American History, a History of Black People in the United States," *Africanaonline,* 10 Jan. 2007 <http://www.africanaonline.com/orga_naacp.htm> par. 2.

as manifested today toward colored people. It takes its name from the fact that the editors believe that this is a critical time in the history of the advancement of men. Catholicity and tolerance, reason and forbearance can today make the world-old dream of human brotherhood approach realization: while bigotry and prejudice, emphasized race consciousness and force can repeat the awful history of the contact of nations and groups in the past. We strive for this higher and broader vision of Peace and Good Will. The policy of *The Crisis* will be simple and well defined: It will first and foremost be a newspaper: it will record important happenings and movements in the world which bear on the great problem of inter-racial relations and especially those which affect the Negro-American.

Secondly, it will be a review of opinion and literature, recording briefly books, articles, and important expressions of opinion in the white and colored press on the race problem. Thirdly, it will publish a few short articles. Finally, its editorial page will stand for the right of men, irrespective of color or race, for the highest ideals of American democracy, and for reasonable but earnest and persistent attempt to gain these rights and realize these ideals. The Magazine will be the organ of no clique or party and will avoid personal rancor of all sorts. In the absence of proof to the contrary it will assume honesty of purpose on the part of all men, North and South, white and black. - *W. E. B. Du Bois*[21]

Within three years, the NAACP established several branch offices including offices in Boston, Massachusetts, Kansas City, Washington D.C., and Detroit. In addition, it opened a branch office in St. Louis, Missouri. One of its earliest strategies was to establish itself as a force to be reckoned with in the legal arena. To buttress this reputation, the NAACP supported, financed, and assisted in legal battles to secure the rights of blacks. One of the first large victories the NAACP won was getting a court to overturn a law that rewarded discrimination in Oklahoma. The law used a grandfather clause to regulate voting. The NAACP thus launched its legalistic strategy. Fresh from legal victories in 1915, the organization began crafting and deploying a public rela-

---

[21] W. E. B. Du Bois, "Opinion," *The Crisis* (Nov. 1910).

tions strategy. This was necessary because the NAACP knew that the proper execution of such a strategy would be critical to its growth and acceptance by blacks as well as liberal whites. The crux of the strategy was that if it could get enough attention turned on itself and its causes, then it would be able to recruit more members and more support as it continued its work toward equality for blacks. "The fledgling organization also learned to harness the power of publicity through its 1915 battle against D. W. Griffith's inflammatory *The Birth of a Nation*, a motion picture that perpetuated demeaning stereotypes of blacks and glorified the Ku Klux Klan."[22]

During this time, the membership of the NAACP grew rapidly and exponentially. In 1917, the NAACP had approximately 9,000 members; two years later it had added almost 100,000 members to its rosters across the nation. The offices grew as well and by 1919 there were more than 300 NAACP offices nationwide. By 1920, the organization had a black secretary named James Weldon Johnson and the first black chairman of the board was elected in 1934. He was a surgeon named Louis T. Wright.[23] From that point forward, these two positions have never again been held by whites. Throughout this time, Du Bois was establishing himself as a noted scholar and thinker and using *The Crisis* as a publication to advocate his views of equality. It became the printed voice for the Harlem renaissance.

In the early years of the NAACP, civil rights were important to the organization; however, human rights were its most pressing concern. By 1920, the NAACP's attention was focused largely on lynchings in America. While the United States pressured the Turkish Ottoman Empire to cease its violence against the Armenians, lynchings continued unhindered in America. Consider this *New York Evening Post* editorial from 1897:

> Mustapha Bey, the Turkish Minister at Washington, will have another chance to score off American sympathizers with the victims of the Sultan. He referred the other day to the Urbana [Ohio] lynching, when asked about Turkish outrages, and now an even more brutal and shocking affair occurred in Maryland.

---

[22] NAACP par. 4.

[23] NAACP.

A Negro actually under sentence of death is taken from the officers of the law and kicked and strangled to death in broad daylight by an infuriated mob, not one man of who even deigned to disguise himself. The judge who had just sentenced the criminal to death rushes out to implore the mob to let the law take its course, but he is lucky to get off himself without lynching. Things are getting worse in the North than in the South; in Virginia they at least let convicted negroes be hanged by process of law; in Maryland the raging mob must slake its thirst for blood without a moment's delay. These occurrences certainly give a queer look to our horror at Armenian massacres. If we content ourselves with protesting against our own lynchings, and disowning them, we are no better than the Sultan, he always protests against his own murderous exploits. If some of the Princess Anne [Maryland] mob can not be brought to justice, why should a sentence of any court, or any law on the statute-book, be any longer respected or heeded in Maryland?[24]

This editorial made clear that the United States was attempting to gain the moral high ground on human rights issues abroad while it continued to ignore the fact that it was engaged in human rights abuses at home. Those human rights violations included the systematic and gratuitous lynching of blacks. The violations also included subjecting blacks to degrading segregation and the denial of human rights strictly on the basis of skin color.

When a bill was proposed that would ensure legal punishment against anyone who participated in a lynching or failed to prosecute those who participated in a lynching, the NAACP provided its unqualified support. "Though the U.S. Congress never passed the bill, or any other anti-lynching legislation, many credit the resulting public debate—fueled by the NAACP's report, *Thirty Years of Lynching in the United States, 1889–1919*—with drastically decreasing the incidence of lynching."[25]

---

[24] *New York Evening Post*, Editorial, 3 Oct. 1897.

[25] *New York Evening Post.*

Sensing an opportunity to engage the international community in its struggle for human rights, the NAACP began to plot its strategy to bring the issue of human rights to the United Nations.

> The Justice Department's *laissez-faire* attitude, juxtaposed to the U.S. government's vigorous prosecution of Nazi war criminals, added fuel to the resentment and frustration burning in the black community. For many, it was sheer 'lipocrisy' for the United States to flex its moral muscle at Nuremberg while claiming impotence in Monroe, Georgia.[26]

Despite a loud and vociferous international critique of American apartheid, its failure to respect black human rights and its continued decision to use the myth of black inferiority to justify rampant human rights abuse, America used its political clout to turn the human rights spotlight away from it and towards the rest of the world. The NAACP exercised its political agency in such a way that the result was the abject failure to raise marginalization and deprivation of black rights to the level of international human rights violations. This decision raised questions. First, was the leadership so dysfunctional that it had lost the desire to chase human rights? Did political reality trump the quest for diuturnal remedies that would address how blacks were actually experiencing racism? Second, was the leadership resigned to the fact that winning civil rights was better than fighting for full human rights, since winning civil rights would at least provide blacks with more rights than they had? Third, did the leadership buy into the notion held by many whites at the time that given their prolonged enslavement blacks could not handle human rights and thus would become wards of the state? This decision to choose civil rights, the path of least resistance, despite its political expediency, was remarkably shortsighted and has had far-reaching and devastating effects on the fight for substantive black equality. It also portended a weakened, chastened, and disjointed organization. The NAACP's disorganization would begrime its image, call into question its relevance, and create an internal culture of organizational paroxysms that continues into the present day.

---

[26] Anna Eleanor Roosevelt, "Why I Do Not Choose to Run," *Look,* 9 Jul. 1946 (Anna Eleanor Roosevelt Papers, Franklin D. Roosevelt Library, Hyde Park, New York).

Combining the white philanthropic support that characterized
Booker T. Washington's accommodationist organizations with
the call for racial justice delivered by W. E. B. Du Bois' militant Niagara Movement, the NAACP forged a middle road of
interracial cooperation. Throughout its existence it has worked
primarily through the American legal system to fulfill its goals
of full suffrage and other civil rights, and an end to segregation
and racial violence. Since the end of the Civil Rights Movement of the 1950s and 1960s, however, the influence of the
NAACP has waned, and it has suffered declining membership
and a series of internal scandals.[27]

[27] *New York Evening Post.*

CHAPTER THREE
THE PERFECT STORM: POLITICS, RACE, AND ECONOMICS

The 1930s were an economically and politically difficult time in America. Given that blacks were still not viewed as full humans, the impact of the great depression was even more profound on them. Statistics show that there was a higher percentage of blacks out of work and living below the poverty level than whites in the same circumstances. In addition to the economic climate of the 1930s, there were serious clashes between the NAACP and the communist party over a collection of issues that had legal, racial, and political overtones.

Perhaps one of the most bitter and public fights between the communist party and the NAACP was the Scottsboro Boys case. In 1931, nine black boys were accused of rape by two white female prostitutes. There was a sham trial and despite evidence of their innocence and evidence which indicated that the prostitutes had invented the story in an effort to avoid prosecution for having traveled across state lines for prostitution, eight of the boys were convicted and all but the youngest were given a sentence of death by the electric chair.[28] Sensing an opportunity to gain a stronghold and win the hearts and minds of blacks, the ILD (the American branch of the communist party) intervened, but the NAACP resisted.

---

[28] Hollace Ransdall, "Report on the Scottsboro, Ala. Case," *Famous American Trials: 'The Scottsboro Boys' Trials 1931–1937*, University of Missouri-Kansas City School of Law, 11 May 2008 <http://www.law.umkc.edu/faculty/projects/FTrials/scottsboro/SB_HRrep.html#Negroes%20Tried%20in%20Four%20Separate%20Cases> par. 10.

While the ILD was a novice in the field of Negro rights, the NAACP had twenty years experience. While the ILD was dominated by communists, the NAACP leadership was liberal and reformist. While the ILD demonstrated concern for the Scottsboro boys with telegrams and ultimatums, the NAACP had demonstrated greater concern earlier. This, at least, was the claim of the NAACP, and it was not to be dismissed lightly. The NAACP, since its inception in 1909, had fought many court battles under the banner of Negro rights. One pertinent instance was the Arkansas riot case (1926), which culminated in a United States Supreme Court ruling that a trial dominated by mob atmosphere is not a trial at all and is, therefore, a violation of due process of law. No Negro organization in America had the power, ability, and respectability of the NAACP. It was the accepted watchtower of Negro rights.

The NAACP maintained that it was the initial defender in the Scottsboro cases. According to Walter White, secretary of the organization, upon news of the arrests near Scottsboro, a number of Negro ministers in Chattanooga, along with the local chapter of the NAACP, stirred to action. Aware of the hostile feelings in Scottsboro, they feared that a Negro lawyer sent to defend the black youths would be ineffective, at best, in saving the lives of the defendants; at worst, ineffective in saving his own life.[29]

Although late to the cause, First Lady Eleanor Roosevelt decided that she would take up the plight of the Negro as her cause celebre.

Though not initially successful, Roosevelt tried to open thousands of jobs to black workers when the NAACP supported labor leader A. Philip Randolph and his march on Washington movement in 1941. Roosevelt also agreed to set up a Fair Employment Practices Committee (FEPC) to ensure compliance.[30]

The NAACP and its leadership were enamored with Eleanor Roosevelt and thought that having the first lady on their side could help

---

[29] Hugh T. Murray, Jr., "The NAACP versus the Communist Party: The Scottsboro Rape Cases, 1931–1932," *Phylon* 28.3 (3rd Qtr., 1967): 279.

[30] *New York Evening Post.*

advance their cause. Things did not go as smoothly as some would have expected. "The black leadership was 'so determined' to break Jim Crow that even 'friend of the Negro' First Lady Eleanor Roosevelt was ignored."[31]

In 1945, Mrs. Roosevelt became a board member of the NAACP. Her board membership brought additional prestige to the organization and helped the NAACP to grow. The NAACP leadership was confused between formal and substantive equality. Formal equality was what whites wanted. They wanted to pass laws that would ostensibly outlaw discrimination, yet still allow discrimination. Formal equality is aspirational and theoretical. What blacks needed was substantive equality, which would ensure that the laws were equal in theory and application. Mrs. Roosevelt's philosophical commitment to limited equality for blacks (formal equality) is captured in her own words to the NAACP:

> Believe, of course, that for our own good in this country, the Negro race as a whole must improve its standards of living, and become both economically and intellectually of higher caliber. The fact that the colored people, not only in the South, but in the North as well, have been economically at a low level, has meant that they have also been physically and intellectually at a low level. Economic conditions are responsible for poor health in children. And the fact that tuberculosis and pneumonia and many other diseases have taken a heavier toll amongst our colored groups can be attributed primarily to economic conditions. It is undoubtedly true that with an improvement in economic condition it will still be necessary not only to improve our educational conditions for children, but to pay special attention to adult education along the line of better living. For you cannot expect people to change overnight, when they have had poor conditions, and adjust themselves to all that we expect of people living as they *should* live today throughout our country.[32]

[31] Roi Ottley, *New World A'Coming: Inside Black America* (Boston: Houghton Mifflin, Life-in-America Books, 1943) 289.

[32] Eleanor Roosevelt, "The Negro and Social Change: A Speech before the National Urban League," *Opportunity* (Jan. 1936): 22–23. (See

Despite her commitment to formal equality, Mrs. Roosevelt's brand helped the NAACP to become so successful in its endeavors that it continued to gain popularity and by 1946 had more than half a million members. It was during this time, however, that it began to move away from human rights and began framing a very narrow civil rights agenda. While it still worked against lynchings and pushed, though not with much success, for anti-lynching laws, it also pushed to end state mandated segregation throughout the nation.

> The Civil Rights Movement of the 1950s and 1960s echoed the NAACP's moderate, integrationist goals but leaders such as Martin Luther King, Jr., of the Southern Christian Leadership Conference (SCLC), felt that direct action was needed to obtain them. Though the NAACP was opposed to extralegal popular actions, many of its members, such as Mississippi Field Secretary Medgar Evers, participated in nonviolent demonstrations such as sit-ins to protest the persistence of Jim Crow segregation throughout the South. Although it was criticized for working exclusively within the system by pursuing legislative and judicial solutions, the NAACP did provide legal representation and aid to members of more militant protest groups.[33]

Beginning in the 1960s and continuing to the present day, the NAACP has focused on a civil rights strategy that is legal in nature and domestic in application. That is, it is not advocating for the vast majority of rights enumerated in the Universal Declaration of Human Rights. It is instead focused on preserving hard fought civil rights victories won in American courts that affect blacks in America. The NAACP demonstrates the fundamental problem with limited political thinking steeped in short-term gains. While it understood that blacks needed both human and civil rights, its own internal political decision making made it choose the path of least resistance. Politics took precedence over policy. Moreover, internal rhubarb took precedence over the human rights of blacks and the very real possibility that the fight for the human rights

---

also Speech and Article File, Anna Eleanor Roosevelt Papers, Franklin D. Roosevelt Library, Hyde Park, New York).

[33] *New York Evening Post.*

of blacks in America would subject the United States to opprobrium on the international stage, and challenge its self-anointed "moral superiority." Thus came the death knell of the NAACP's fight for human rights. The nail in the coffin for black human rights in America was driven by 'friend of the Negro' and NAACP board member Eleanor Roosevelt. This was not a surprise. In an article she wrote for *Ebony Magazine* entitled "Some of My Best Friends are Negro," she talked about Paul Robeson, the black author and civil rights activist, whose appearance on her show was cancelled and whose recordings were taken out of circulation because he was accused of being a communist:

> I don't think I have ever lost a Negro friend. One that I could have lost had we been friends would have been Paul Robeson, but I never really knew him. I had a great admiration for him as an artist. I was once told the story of his youth and I held him in high regard. I deeply regret that because of his gratitude to the Russian people for giving him what he thought that he wanted, he had allowed himself to be fooled by the kind of life that he was able to lead there. I think he has done his people and my good friends a disservice. In a way, he has misused his great talent to do this. It is too bad, because he should be using his talents to help rather than destroy his country. Despite his intelligence, I feel that he has not demonstrated any analytical qualities. Surely he has not examined the Soviet system, because it does not permit real democratic freedom. The kindest thing that I can say about him, is perhaps, that he believes that communism will give all people equality. This everyone should have. But Mr. Robeson and all of us have a greater chance of getting it here in the U.S. than anywhere else in the world.[34]

As she wrote disparagingly of Robeson, did she consider that Robeson did in fact use his analytical skills and determined that the U.S. was engaging in a systemic pattern of human rights abuses against blacks and that some blacks had simply grown tired of it? Did she consider that whites already had equality and so the "all of us" she spoke

---

[34] Eleanor Roosevelt, "Some of My Best Friends are Negro," originally printed in *Ebony* 9 (February 1953): 16-20, 22, 24-26, 13 Aug. 2008 <http://newdeal.feri.org/er/er09.htm> par. 49.

of did not include whites? What responsibility did the whites who had destroyed the "souls of black folks" have to their country, which lay in racial ruins? Was she suggesting that America was the paragon of real democratic freedom? If so, how was real democratic freedom squared with the reality of legalized racial discrimination? Did real democracy have its limits? If so, did those limits apply only to blacks? Who did these limits benefit? It seems the NAACP's leadership failed to ask her these questions, and therefore got no answers. Perhaps they believed that her presence alone would be sufficient to topple the shameful racial democracy that was America.

CHAPTER FOUR
COMMUNISM, RACE-BAITING, AND BACK-BITING

I turn now to an examination of some of the key players in the NAACP in an effort to shed light on their roles in shaping the NAACP's civil rights strategy. The more controversial key players were instrumental in the decision by the NAACP to move toward civil rights and away from human rights. One of the obstacles that the NAACP had to overcome in the 1940s and 1950s was the fact that at least some of its members and leaders were actively working with communist organizations.

> The Cold War, McCarthyism, the Soviets' atomic explosion, and the Korean War, unleashed a maelstrom of fear, xenophobia, and conformity that wreaked havoc across America's political and progressive landscape. Public enemy No.1 was of course the Communist Party USA and its supporters.[35]

For those who opposed the NAACP, the ability to link the organization with communism provided the smoke and mirrors needed to challenge the relevance and efficacy of the organization. Prior to being painted with the "red brush of communism," the NAACP was well on its way to a sustained human rights strategy. It was one of the political realties that undoubtedly caused the organization to move toward the protection of constitutional civil rights and away from more vaguely guarded and protected human rights. Scholars have also noted that for-

---

[35] Carol Anderson, *Eyes off the Prize: The United Nations and the African American Struggle for Human Rights, 1944–1955* (Cambridge, UK: Cambridge University Press) 166.

eign policy concerns led the federal government to utilize public relations exercises to challenge claims about American racism.[36] Furthermore, the domestic "red scare" that gathered force in the late 1940s and
early 1950s tarred any criticism of American inequalities with the brush
of communism, and anti-communist attacks and investigations deci-
mated the American left. Civil rights opponents, including the FBI, red-
baited, investigated, and harassed civil rights organizations, destroying
the Civil Rights Congress (CRC).

In December of 1951, Paul Robeson and William Patterson
submit a petition titled, '*We Charge Genocide: The Crime of
Government Against the Negro People*' to the United Nations.
This book-length petition documents hundreds of lynching
cases and a clear pattern of government inaction or actual
complicity. It charges that in the 85 years since the end of
slavery more than 10,000 Blacks were *known* to have been
lynched (on average, more than 100 per year), and that the full
number would never be known because the murders were often
unreported. The petition cites the UN's definition of genocide:
'Any intent to destroy, *in whole or in part*, a national, racial, or
religious group is genocide.' The petition concludes therefore,
that '[. . .] the oppressed Negro citizens of the United States,
segregated, discriminated against, and long the target of violence, suffer from genocide as the result of the consistent, conscious, unified policies of every branch of government. If the
General Assembly acts as the conscience of mankind and
therefore acts favorably on our petition, it will have served the
cause of peace.' With the McCarthyite 'Red Scare' and the
'Cold War' raging, the U.S. government immediately moves to
prevent the United Nations from considering the charges
brought in the petition. Working behind the scenes, they are
able to prevent any discussion of the petition by the UN Commission on Human Rights. When one of the American dele-
gates to the UN criticizes William Patterson for 'attacking your
government,' Patterson replies, 'It's your government. It's my
country. I am fighting to save my country's democratic princi-

---

[36] Mark Newman, "Civil Rights and Human Rights," *Reviews in
American History* 32.2 (Jun 2004): 247–254.

ples.' For this and other actions that challenge the status quo, both Robeson and Patterson (founder and leader of the Civil Rights Congress), are persecuted and harassed by the FBI and State Department throughout the 1950s.[37]

The scourge of communism encouraged the NAACP to adopt a strict anti-communist policy. As Professor Mary L. Dudziak explains: "The narrow boundaries of Cold War-era civil rights politics kept discussions of broad-based social change, or a linking of race and class, off the agenda."[38]

> The internal witch-hunt in the NAACP was ruthless. Roy Wilkins and a resurrected Walter White, vowed to clean out the NAACP and make sure that Communists were not running it. So fervent were White and his allies to rid the NAACP of its communist ties, they rigged the elections in the San Francisco branch to oust its left-leaning president, and limited support for the victims of the government's loyalty program to those whose patriotism had been questioned solely because of race or membership in the NAACP.[39]

McCarthyism made advocates of human rights through the UN vulnerable to accusations of communism and therefore restricted the agenda of the black struggle to the narrow field of civil rights pursued by the NAACP. The CRC and the Council on African Affairs, both communist influenced, fell victim to federal government harassment and dissolved in the mid-1950s. As a purely political matter, incoming republican President Dwight D. Eisenhower had little commitment to civil rights. In addition, there was a growing conservative chorus which suggested that America was ceding its sovereignty to foreign governments. In an attempt to address this issue, members of Congress introduced the Bricker Amendment.

---

[37] William L. Patterson, ed., *We Charge Genocide*, (New York: International Publishers, 1970) 25.

[38] Mary L. Dudziak, *Cold War Civil Rights: Race and the Image of American Democracy* (Princeton U, 2000) 13.

[39] Clarence Mitchell, Letter to Louis E. Hosch, 1 Mar. 1950, Box H126, File "Loyalty Review Cases, 1947–1951."

Introduced into the Senate in February 1952, as Senate Joint Resolution 130, the Bricker Amendment to the Constitution read as follows:

- Section 1. A provision of a treaty which conflicts with this Constitution shall not be of any force or effect.
- Section 2. A treaty shall become effective as internal law in the United States only through legislation which would be valid in the absence of treaty.
- Section 3. Congress shall have power to regulate all executive and other agreements with any foreign power or international organization. All such agreements shall be subject to the limitations imposed on treaties by this article.
- Section 4. The congress shall have power to enforce this article by appropriate legislation.

Eisenhower opposed the Bricker Amendment because he believed that it would have severely restricted the executive branch's ability to conduct foreign policy. Sensing growing support for the amendment, he became concerned. In an effort to head off southern democrat and republican support for it,[40] Eisenhower promised that he would ensure that there was no American support for a UN genocide convention and covenants on human rights or political and civil rights, despite the NAACP's opposition. The NAACP supported the covenants as well as the convention, because they viewed these as avenues through which they could bring America to task internationally. Eisenhower would have none of it. He further made his position on racial issues clear by successfully nominating strongly avowed racist James F. Byrnes to the United States delegation to the UN. Former communist leader Yergan, by now an FBI informant, castigated Walter White for opposing Byrnes's nomination and blasted White as a communist. White replied in kind; however, the NAACP's vigorous anti-communist stance and avowals of patriotism did not save NAACP members from accusations of disloyalty.

One of the most prominent figures in the early days of the NAACP was of course W. E. B. Du Bois. Du Bois was considered one of the founders of the organization and he worked hard for the equality of

---

[40] Duane Tananbaum, "The Bricker Amendment Controversy: A Test of Eisenhower's Political Leadership," *Amer. Hist. Rev.* 95.1 (1990): 289.

blacks. However, his ties to and affection for communism would ultimately hurt the organization. Although initially an asset to the organization, his uncompromising style, big ego, and written missives casti-
gating the NAACP would ultimately lead to his ouster from both the
NAACP and Atlanta University.

As an adult, W. E. B. Du Bois was labeled a radical. Du Bois did
not consider the radical label to be a pejorative; it was instead a badge
of honor that he wore with pride. History judges Du Bois in a number
of ways. Du Bois is remembered not only as a radical and someone
who created a great deal of consternation within the NAACP, he is also
remembered as someone with a keen intellect, who paid attention to
details, and had a passion for human rights. He was considered brilliant
by many, including those who did not agree with his views.

> His singular greatness lay in his quest for truth about his own
> people. There were very few scholars who concerned them-
> selves with honest study of the black man and he sought to fill
> this immense void. The degree to which he succeeded dis-
> closed the great dimensions of the man.[41]

Understanding how he came to be the man that he was and how he
came to impact the decision of the NAACP to move toward civil rights
instead of human rights as a platform is more readily accomplished
when one contextualizes his upbringing.

W. E. B. Du Bois was born on Feb. 23, 1868 in Massachusetts.
Had he been born in the South he may have been raised to be completely subservient to the whites that surrounded him; however, because he was born in the North he was raised to be a man without actually being given the privilege. Being born in the North provided him
with a lifestyle in which he could attain education, but it had to be from
a black school, and he could eat out as long as he sat at the segregated
lunch counters. He was allowed many "privileges" that his peers in the
South would not have been entitled to during that historical period. The
town in which he was raised had a population of about 5,000. Of those
5,000 people, it is estimated that fewer than 50 were black.[42] He did not

[41] Gerald C. Hynes, *Biographical Sketch of W. E. B. Du Bois,* 10 May
2008 <http://www.duboislc.org/html/DuBoisBio.html> par. 1.

[42] Hynes.

encounter a lot of overt and obvious acts of racism as a child in that town. He was a bright child and he later noted that he remembered hearing many innuendos that he was inferior to whites because he was black. It was something he did not accept, since his family had raised him to believe that he could do what he wanted through hard work and determination. However, his almost continuous encounters with subtle, and sometimes overt, forms of racism had a profound impact on him, his politics, and his view of race and racism. Some say it is why he would later be described as withdrawn and angry.[43]

> Among the Negroes of Great Harrington, young Will DuBois soon came to have a very special place. He was the only Negro in his high-school class of twelve and one of the two or three boys in the whole class who went on to college. After school and on weekends he worked at all sorts of jobs. Through his friendship with the local newsdealer, he obtained, for a brief period, a position as local correspondent for the Springfield Republican. He also contributed local news to two Negro newspapers, one in Boston and the other in New York. With a few harsh exceptions as he reached adolescence, he was accepted on his merits by his peers. Though not particularly good at sports, he was highly respected intellectually. At fifteen, he began annotating his collected papers, a practice he scrupulously followed until his death, in Ghana, at the age of ninety-five. [44]

He was intellectually gifted and he enjoyed surpassing his peers in academic endeavors. When he graduated from high school he went on to Fisk University in Nashville. It was the first time the young Du Bois had been south and he was appalled at the way he and other blacks in the area were routinely treated by whites. Once he graduated from Fisk, he pursued graduate studies at Harvard. He focused on history and philosophy and eventually refined his areas of interest to economics, social justice, and the past and present plights of blacks.

---

[43] Kennedy Mkutu, "A Critical Analysis of the Contributions of Notable Black Economists," *Economic Affairs* 25.1 (2005): 63–64.

[44] E. Digby Baltzell, introduction, *A Social Study*, by W. E. B. Du Bois (New York: Shocken Books, 1967) xi.

Du Bois graduated from Harvard and then studied abroad in Germany. He later returned to Harvard and earned his PhD with a doctoral thesis entitled, "The Suppression of the African Slave Trade in America."[45] While at Harvard, he wrote:

> By good fortune, I was thrown into direct contact with many of these men. I was repeatedly a guest in the house of William James; he was my friend and guide to clear thinking; I was a member of the Philosophical Club and talked with Royce and Palmer; I sat in an upper room and read Kant's Critique with Santayana; Shaler invited a Southerner, who objected to sitting by me, out of his class; I became one of Hart's favorite pupils and was afterwards guided by him through my graduate course and started on my work in Germany. It was a great opportunity for a young man and a young American Negro, and I realized it.[46]

He became a teacher and began to study the plight of blacks from a sociological perspective. This approach undergirded his research and scholarly pursuits. "He was certain that the race problem was one of ignorance. And he was determined to unearth as much knowledge as he could, thereby providing the 'cure' for color prejudice."[47]

He also taught at the University of Pennsylvania. Of his time there he wrote:

> In the fall of 1896, I went to the University of Pennsylvania as 'Assistant Instructor' in Sociology. It all happened this way: Philadelphia, then and still one of the worst governed of America's badly governed cities, was having one of its periodic spasms of reform. A thorough study of causes was called for. Not but what the underlying cause was evident to most white Philadelphians: the corrupt, semi-criminal vote of the Negro Seventh Ward, Everyone agreed that here lay the cancer; but

---

[45] W. E. B. Du Bois, *The Suppression of the African Slave Trade to the United States of America, 1638–1870*, diss., Harvard (New York: Longmans, 1904).

[46] W. E. B. Du Bois, *Dusk of Dawn: An Essay Toward an Autobiography of a Race Concept* (1940; New York: Schocken Books, 1968) 34.

[47] Hynes par. 15.

would it not be well to elucidate the known causes by a scientific investigation, with the imprimatur of the University? It certainly would, answered Samuel McCune Lindsay of the Department of Sociology. And he put his finger on me for the task. There must have been some opposition, for the invitation was not particularly cordial. I was offered a salary of $800 for a limited period of one year. I was given no real academic standing, no office at the University, no official recognition of any kind; my name was even eventually omitted from the catalogue; I had no contact with students, and very little with members of the faculty, even in my department. With my bride of three months, I settled in one room over a cafeteria run by a College Settlement, in the worst part of the Seventh Ward. We lived there a year, in the midst of an atmosphere of dirt, drunkenness, poverty and crime. Murder sat on our doorsteps, police were our government, and philanthropy dropped in with periodic advice.[48]

His research and writings appeared in several publications. At the same time, the more involved he became the angrier he grew about the way blacks were being treated in America. He then spent 13 years at Atlanta University as a teacher and writer.

During this period an ideological controversy grew between Du Bois and Booker T. Washington, which later grew into a bitter personal battle. When he made his famous 'Atlanta Compromise' speech, in 1910, he was arguably the most powerful black man in America. This was evidenced by the fact that any time whites received a grant or other research funding on the issue of racism and black life, he was often asked to approve or reject such projects. Hence, the 'Tuskegee Machine' became the focal point for black input/output. Du Bois was not opposed to Washington's power, but rather, he was against his ideology/methodology of handling the power.[49]

---

[48] Rayford Logan, *The Negro in the United States: A Brief History* (Princeton, New Jersey: Van Nostrand, 1957) 54.

[49] Hynes par. 16.

Shortly after 1905, Du Bois began his involvement with the NAACP. His intelligence was considered a positive contribution to the organization and his ability to write and edit were an asset. As director of *The Crisis,* his editorial philosophy and writings were often controversial. For example, He called for resistance against attempts being made by whites in various cities outside of the South to institute segregated schools.[50] He concluded that "white teachers do not, as a rule love or sympathize with their poor little black charges, and that the white board engaged only submissive Negro teachers."[51] He also encouraged "enterprising" artisans and professionals to migrate to the Northwest and he volunteered to answer all inquires about that area.[52] After some white men insulted white and Negro marchers in a suffrage parade, he wrote:

> Wasn't it glorious? Does it not make you burn with shame to be a mere Black man when such mighty deeds are done by the Leaders of Civilization? Does it make you ashamed of your race?' Does it not make you 'want to be white?'[53]

His editorials did not always sit well with others in the NAACP and there were many arguments and heated power battles between Du Bois and other members of the organization. It was the beginning of the internal struggles that the organization would experience that contributed to the decision to move toward civil rights and abandon human rights.

Du Bois always objected to having whites occupy positions of power within the NAACP. He believed that whites should play supporting roles in the NAACP if they were to play any roles at all. Other members of the organization, including Booker T. Washington, disagreed with him. At the same time, a simmering battle began between Du Bois and Walter White, the executive secretary of the NAACP and

---

[50] Robert L. Harris, Jr., "Coming of Age: The Transformation of Afro-American Historiography," *Journal of Negro History* 67.2 (1982): 107–121.

[51] Du Bois Nov. 1910.

[52] W. E. B. Du Bois, "Opinion," *The Crisis* (Nov. 1913).

[53] Du Bois Nov. 1913.

his boss. Ultimately, this would cause White to orchestrate Du Bois' less than graceful exit from the NAACP.

The meteoric and sustained rise in the circulation of *The Crisis,* which made it self-supporting, mollified the moderates within the association and thus gave Du Bois the political cover to continue his assault on the injustices heaped upon blacks. Though Du Bois did create a tense environment for many of the organization's members, the writings that he published managed to meet several of his objectives, including:

- "inaugurating the opening of Black officer training schools.
- bringing forth legal action against lynchers.
- setting up a federal work plan for returning veterans."[54]

Du Bois and White continued to have internal struggles at the NAACP, and eventually these struggles spilled out into public view.

> Du Bois' disagreements with Walter White increased as the financial loses at *The Crisis* increased. White, conscious that NAACP income had dropped during the depression, maintained that the organization's limited resources should be spent on anti-lynching campaigns, court cases, and legislative lobbying. In 1930, after the permanent departure of Executive Secretary James Weldon Johnson, White assumed greater power on the *Crisis* editorial board. Dubois threatened to resign unless the board's composition changed.[55]

White did not budge and the composition of the board stayed the same. White and Du Bois were in fact working together on providing advice and counsel to Mrs. Roosevelt on the UN Declaration on Human Rights. However, "In this setting, Dubois' avowed faith in socialism, his assertions that the difference between communism and socialism and capitalism was 'the difference between heaven and hell,' and his open hostility toward the Truman administration made him a major

---

[54] *New York Evening Post.*

[55] Elliott M. Rudwick, "W. E. B. Du Bois in the Role of Crisis Editor," *The Journal of Negro History* 43.3 (Jul. 1958): 236.

liability."[56] However, White, being the ultimate consensus builder and politician, appeared tailor made for the job.[57] Given Du Bois' intellectual heft, White asked him to comment further on the Universal Declaration of Human Rights. Du Bois refused. He instead decided to deliver a jeremiad on what he considered to be the root cause of the NAACP's floundering human rights policy. According to Du Bois:

> [t]he trail of incompetency and betrayal led directly to Walter White's political machinations. White had 'jump[ed] on the Truman bandwagon' and tied the NAACP to the 'reactionary, war-mongering colonial imperialism of the present administration.' White was apparently rewarded with an all expenses paid trip to Paris for his efforts to bring the black vote to Truman, while Du Bois had received 'five threats and warnings from officials of the NAACP for informing blacks about the only candidate who was honestly committed to black equality.[58]

The memo was seen as intemperate by White and others in the NAACP. However, the fact that it was leaked to *The New York Times* before the board could review it infuriated White. When he confronted Du Bois and asked how it was leaked, Du Bois blamed it on his secretary. White asked the board of the NAACP to oust Du Bois. Some members agreed and others wanted to give him a chance to explain himself.

> Perhaps Du Bois admitted innocently enough, he was ultimately responsible for the leak because he had distributed copies to his staff, as well as to members of the board. At that moment, the board paused. That explanation was plausible. Maybe someone else on the staff not Du Bois, released the memo. Just as the situation was being defused, however, the eloquent Du Bois uttered one phrase too many. He added that if the newspapers had asked him about his memorandum, he would have given it to them because he did not consider the

---

[56] Anderson, *Eyes off the Prize*, 139.

[57] Anderson, *Eyes off the Prize,* 139.

[58] W. E. B. Du Bois, Memo to Walter White, 23 Aug. 1948.

matter a secret. Stunned, one Board member asked him to repeat what he had just said. Du Bois blithely reasserted that 'he
would have given it to the press.' With that incendiary admis-
sion, Du Bois left both the room and his tenure with the
NAACP in ashes.[59]

After making several trips to Africa, he resigned from the NAACP.
His resignation was not voluntary. First, he was an avowed socialist
and this did not sit well with the governing board of the NAACP. Second, he questioned the NAACP's move away from human rights and
towards civil rights. Third, he had an independent streak and he used
The Crisis to express it. Fourth, he and Walter White had clashed both
privately and publicly. Fifth, the leaked memo and his response were
simply unacceptable to a majority of the board. Finally, *The Crisis* was
losing money and so he no longer had the political cover to say and do
as he pleased. As a result of all of this, he left the NAACP and retuned
to the faculty of Atlanta University, bloodied but unbowed.

---

[59] Dudziak 144.

CHAPTER FIVE
HE AIN'T WHITE, HE'S MY BROTHER

A thorough, sifting analysis of the NAACP during the Du Bois-White era reveals that there were many developmental problems in the organization. Among them were: who should be a member, how best to ensure financial stability, and should the focus be on civil and or human rights?[60] However, the most damaging issue that the organization faced was the irreconcilable rift between the socialist Du Bois and the pacifist White.

"White was one of the most important civil rights leaders of the first half of the twentieth century."[61] He had blond hair and blue eyes, which made him look white and not black. It was a point that Du Bois would bring up frequently to point out that White could not possibly truly understand the plight of the blacks in this country because he could easily be mistaken for white and get the benefits of being white by society. White never claimed to be white, however most of his friends and people that he associated with were white.

White came to civil rights work as a result of actions by the Atlanta Board of Education. He discovered that the Board of Education was going to drop seventh-grade public education for all black students so that it could use the money to fund the building of a new school for

---

[60] George Washington University, "Teaching Eleanor Roosevelt Glossary: Walter White (1893–1955)," The Eleanor Roosevelt Papers Project, 10 Mar. 2008 <http://www.gwu.edu/~erpapers/teachinger/glossary/white-walter.cfm>.

[61] George Washington University, "Teaching Eleanor Roosevelt Glossary," par. 1.

white students. To White, this seemed an unconscionable decision. As a result of this, he began a sustained campaign of civil rights protests and advocacy.

He and Du Bois originally worked together on a number of issues related to civil and human rights. Both believed the issue of lynching and its impact on the black population needed to be addressed decisively. They both felt that the government was not doing enough to stop it and both initially agreed to take this issue to the United Nations. While White was a diplomat, Du Bois was a radical; however they were both uncompromising and egocentric. It was their egocentrism and uncompromising approaches that would largely be responsible for the adoption of a civil rights strategy. Walter White and Du Bois were the proverbial oil and water. Their disagreements were personal, vitriolic, and very public.[62]

Perhaps one of the biggest scandals involving White and the NAACP was his decision to leave his black wife and marry Poppy Cannon, a white woman. In 1922 he had married Leah Gladys Powell, a clerical worker in the association's headquarters. They had two children, Jane and Walter. That marriage ended in divorce in 1949, and the same year he married Poppy Cannon, a white woman born in South Africa. There was, of course, salacious gossip that White was seeing Poppy during his marriage and that he left a fine black woman with whom he had children to marry a white woman. The political problem, of course, was that White's decision to marry a white woman played into the hands of the anti-miscegenation hysteria which declared that black men wanted to be "free and equal" for no other purpose than to seek out and sleep with white women.

Within the NAACP, this interracial marriage provoked protests and calls for White's resignation. But White, ever the defender of integration, shrugged off the criticism, maintaining that one's choice of a mate was a private matter. Eleanor Roosevelt, who had joined the association's board of directors after her husband's death, saved White's position by threatening to resign should White be dismissed. Although declining health soon forced him to turn over many of his administrative

---

[62] August Meier and John H. Bracey, Jr., "The NAACP as a Reform Movement, 1909–1965: To Reach the Conscience of America," *The Journal of Southern History* 59.1 (Feb. 1993): 12.

duties to Roy Wilkins, he remained the NAACP's executive secretary and most important public spokesperson until his death in 1955.[63, 64]

Walter White was an important figure in the NAACP, but was his concern the formal removal of barriers without an equal emphasis on ensuring that racism and marginalization were eradicated at their core? Did he consider the ultimate sign of his success his ability to marry a white woman? Was he about progress or gate keeping? Was he the acceptable Negro? Did his model of leadership during this turbulent era create a model for black men such as Ward Connerly? Perhaps Walter White's approach finds itself in black leaders who depend so heavily on whites for approval that they forget that the struggle for equality is not a mere intellectual abstraction. Equality in a racialized America can only be won when we understand that addressing racism requires that we acknowledge the role that we as blacks play in colluding with racists at the expense of true equality and to the detriment of ourselves.

---

[63] George Washington University, "Teaching Eleanor Roosevelt Glossary."

[64] Georgia Humanities Council and the University of Georgia Press, "Walter White," 2008, *The New Georgia Encyclopedia*, 10 May 2008 <http://www.georgiaencyclopedia.org/nge/Article.jsp?id=h-747>.

CHAPTER SIX
YEZ UM MS. ROOSEVELT

Eleanor Roosevelt[65] came late to the issue of black equality. Before she arrived at the White House, it was reported that issues of race did not dominate her thinking and perhaps seldom even enter her thinking. Of course this was common for whites at that time, for whom the issue of racism was largely intellectual. The fact that she was the first lady made her no different. As first lady, she decided that the issues of discrimination against blacks, segregation, and lynchings were issues she would address. It was on her travels of the nation during the Great Depression that her education about what was actually happening to blacks in America came to the fore.

> And although she had visited blacks when she toured poverty stricken areas the summer after she became First Lady, she did not recognize the depth of institutional racism until she pressured the Subsistence Homestead Administration to admit blacks to Arthurdale.[66]

---

[65] Eleanor Roosevelt served three separate, but important roles in the fight for civil and human rights: first lady, NAACP board chair, and chair of the U.N. Commission on Human Rights. She obviously did not serve them all at the same time. The impact of her influence cannot be ignored.

[66] George Washington University, "Eleanor Roosevelt and Civil Rights," *The Eleanor Roosevelt Papers Project*, 10 Mar. 2008 <http://www.gwu.edu/~erpapers/teachinger/lesson-plans/notes-er-and-civil -rights.cfm> par. 2.

Although she was unsuccessful in her first civil rights efforts, she later invited NAACP Executive Secretary Walter White to the White House to talk about the situation and brainstorm solutions with her. Following that meeting, the first lady began to pressure the National Recovery Administration into explaining why there were different wages for blacks and whites performing the same jobs in some of the southern industries. She even confronted the armed services and questioned the racial climate that ensured whites were provided training that made them employable post navy while blacks were being assigned jobs that permanently trapped them at the bottom of the post navy employment ladder in which they were cooks, cleaners, and dishwashers. To be sure, her position as first lady allowed her access to information and influence on policy that she would not have had otherwise.

Although she appeared to have the interests of blacks in mind, like other whites of the time, she embraced contradictory positions. She in fact seemed to embrace policy that accepted segregation but demanded equality within that system. In other words, she accepted the farcical position of "separate but equal." She viewed the NAACP as a vehicle by which she could push a civil rights agenda. She knew that the organization would not always agree with her, but she could use it and the organization could use her. It seemed the perfect symbiotic relationship.

Like so many at the time, her civil rights agenda was aimed at broad objectives such as housing and education. On the issue of education, she found her voice. For her, education seemed the ultimate civil right and one that she embraced with strength and clout. When she was invited to speak at the Conference on Negro Education she told participants that "wherever the standard of education is low, the standard of living is low" and urged states to address the inequities in public school funding.[67] The vigor and passion with which she spoke on education earned her hero status by many in the increasingly influential press and the black community. By early 1934 she was lionized by the black press and was touted to be the "ultimate friend to the Negro." She would soon forge an alliance with Mary McLeod Bethune, a lioness of black education and founder of Bethune Cookman College, which edu-

---

[67] George Washington University, "Eleanor Roosevelt and Civil Rights," par. 2.

cated Negroes. With Bethune in tow, Roosevelt's credibility with large segments of the black community soared.

> Mary McLeod Bethune, whom Eleanor Roosevelt had met in 1927 at an education conference and whom she urged be appointed to the National Youth Administration in 1935, also helped shape her understanding of the problems facing black Americans. She brought lists of requests for her intervention when the two met and often sent reports, novels, and other reading material to her attention.[68]

The two women became very close friends and it was this friendship that Eleanor Roosevelt credits with helping her finally release her age-old viewpoints and embrace true equality.

While President Roosevelt dealt with Mrs. Roosevelt's focus and interests without much comment, when she chose to support the efforts of the NAACP to pass an anti-lynching bill he became infuriated. His anger increased when his wife showed public support for the bill by attending an art show about lynching. Her actions in support of the NAACP created rumors nationwide that she was contaminated with black blood. The American public was not ready to believe that a white first lady would so publicly defy her husband and support the NAACP in all its efforts, so it assumed that the rumors had to be true. The head of the FBI, J. Edgar Hoover, was so offended by her support of blacks that he too began to insist she had to be part black to have such an interest in their rights and needs[69]. The rumors were further spurred when a friend wrote her a letter asking her about the rumor and she replied that her family had been in America for so long there was no way for her to answer that question with any certainty.[70]

At this point, Eleanor Roosevelt had done a great deal to support the efforts of the NAACP. She had effectively used her role as first lady to advance the cause. For this, most of the organization was grateful. Most members relished the clout and cache she brought to the or-

---

[68] George Washington University, "Eleanor Roosevelt and Civil Rights," par. 5.

[69] Athan G. Theoharis and John Stuart Cox, T*he Boss: J. Edgar Hoover and the Great American Inquisition* (Philadelphia: Temple UP, 1988).

[70] Theoharis and Cox.

ganization. Her efforts, however, were focused on civil rights. The NAACP was so happy that she was taking up many of its causes that it did not examine Eleanor Roosevelt the politician. In addition, the leadership of the NAACP seemed to forget that race had been socially constructed and ingrained in the minds of blacks and whites in America. Eradicating racism meant challenging an entrenched hegemonic power structure that Mrs. Roosevelt could not or would not confront. Eleanor Roosevelt was an icon of white privilege who could do little to deconstruct hegemonic and binary construction of race without first acknowledging and acting to remove her own white privilege. There is no evidence that she did so. Of Walter White of the NAACP she wrote:

> He has suffered often I fear and I remember one story which shows the kind of loyalty he has to his race. One time he said he was washing his hands in the Senate washroom, I think. One of the senators came in and asked him: 'why do you insist on being a Negro?' Walter's response was so simple and so self-embracing. He said 'Because I am a Negro.' He is as fair as any Nordic and I can see how it is difficult to consider him a Negro, but he told me his father was unmistakably colored.[71]

Her friendship with Mary McLeod Bethune may have softened her views on race, but not on white privilege.

The fundamental problem with whites and their understanding of racism and its effects is that so many whites fail to recognize or accept what Peggy McIntosh has identified and explained as the unearned privilege that comes with whiteness.

> Through work to bring materials from women's studies into the rest of the curriculum, I have often noticed men's unwillingness to grant that they are overprivileged, even though they may grant that women are disadvantaged. They may say they will work to improve women's status, in the society, the university, or the curriculum, but they can't or won't support the idea of lessening men's. Denials that amount to taboos surround the subject of advantages that men gain from women's disadvantages. These denials protect male privilege from being fully acknowledged, lessened, or ended.

---

[71] Roosevelt, "Some of My Best Friends are Negro," 28.

Thinking through unacknowledged male privilege as a phenomenon, I realized that, since hierarchies in our society are interlocking, there was most likely a phenomenon of white privilege that was similarly denied and protected. As a white person, I realized I had been taught about racism as something that puts others at a disadvantage, but had been taught not to see one of its corollary aspects, white privilege, which puts me at an advantage.

I think whites are carefully taught not to recognize white privilege, as males are taught not to recognize male privilege. So I have begun in an untutored way to ask what it is like to have white privilege. I have come to see white privilege as an invisible package of unearned assets that I can count on cashing in each day, but about which I was 'meant' to remain oblivious. White privilege is like an invisible weightless knapsack of special provisions, maps, passports, codebooks, visas, clothes, tools, and blank checks.

Describing white privilege makes one newly accountable. As we in women's studies work to reveal male privilege and ask men to give up some of their power, so one who writes about having white privilege must ask, 'having described it, what will I do to lessen or end it?'

After I realized the extent to which men work from a base of unacknowledged privilege, I understood that much of their oppressiveness was unconscious. Then I remembered the frequent charges from women of color that white women whom they encounter are oppressive. I began to understand why we are justly seen as oppressive, even when we don't see ourselves that way. I began to count the ways in which I enjoy unearned skin privilege and have been conditioned into oblivion about its existence.

My schooling gave me no training in seeing myself as an oppressor, as an unfairly advantaged person, or as a participant in a damaged culture. I was taught to see myself as an individual whose moral state depended on her individual moral will. My schooling followed the pattern my colleague Elizabeth Minnich has pointed out: whites are taught to think of their lives as morally neutral, normative, and average, and also ideal, so that when we work to benefit others, this is seen as work that will allow 'them' to be more like 'us.' [. . .] I want, then, to distinguish between earned strength and unearned power conferred systematically. Power from unearned privilege can look like strength when it is in fact permission to escape or to dominate. But not all of the privileges on my list are inevitably damaging. Some, like the expectation that neighbors will be decent to you, or that your race will not count against you in court, should be the norm in a just society. Others, like the privilege to ignore less powerful people, distort the humanity of the holders as well as the ignored groups.

We might at least start by distinguishing between positive advantages, which we can work to spread, and negative types of advantages, which unless rejected will always reinforce our present hierarchies. For example, the feeling that one belongs within the human circle, as Native Americans say, should not be seen as privilege for a few. Ideally it is an unearned entitlement. At present, since only a few have it, it is an unearned advantage for them. This paper results from a process of coming to see that some of the power that I originally saw as attendant on being a human being in the United States consisted in unearned advantage and conferred dominance.

I have met very few men who are truly distressed about systemic, unearned male advantage and conferred dominance. And so one question for me and others like me is whether we will be like them, or whether we will get truly distressed, even outraged, about unearned race advantage and conferred dominance, and, if so, what we will do to lessen them. In any case, we need to do more work in identifying how they actually affect our daily lives. Many, perhaps most, of our white students in the United States think that racism doesn't affect them because they are not people of color; they do not see 'whiteness' as a racial identity. In addition, since race and sex are not the only advantaging systems at work, we need similarly to examine the daily experience of having age advantage, or ethnic advantage, or physical ability, or advantage related to nationality, religion, or sexual orientation.

Difficulties and dangers surrounding the task of finding parallels are many. Since racism, sexism, and heterosexism are not the same, the advantages associated with them should not be seen as the same. In addition, it is hard to disentangle aspects of unearned advantage that rest more on social class, economic class, race, religion, sex, and ethnic identity than on other factors. Still, all of the oppressions are interlocking, as the members of the Combahee River Collective pointed out in their 'Black Feminist Statement' of 1977.

One factor seems clear about all of the interlocking oppressions. They take both active forms, which we can see, and embedded forms, which as a member of the dominant groups one is taught not to see. In my class and place, I did not see myself as a racist because I was taught to recognize racism only in individual acts of meanness by members of my group, never in invisible systems conferring unsought racial dominance on my group from birth.

Disapproving of the system won't be enough to change them. I was taught to think that racism could end if white individuals changed their attitude. But a 'white' skin in the United States opens many doors for whites whether or not we approve of the way dominance has been conferred on us. Individual acts can palliate, but cannot end, these problems.

To redesign social systems we need first to acknowledge their colossal unseen dimensions. The silences and denials surrounding privilege are the key political tool here. They keep the thinking about equality or equity incomplete, protecting unearned advantage and conferred dominance by making these subjects taboo. Most talk by whites about equal opportunity seems to me now to be about equal opportunity to try to get into a position of dominance while denying that systems of dominance exist.

It seems to me that obliviousness about white advantage, like obliviousness about male advantage, is kept strongly inculturated in the United States so as to maintain the myth of meritocracy, the myth that democratic choice is equally available to all. Keeping most people unaware that freedom of confident action is there for just a small number of people props up those in power and serves to keep power in the hands of the same groups that have most of it already.

Although systemic change takes many decades, there are pressing questions for me and, I imagine, for some others like me if we raise our daily consciousness on the perquisites of being light-skinned. What will we do with such knowledge? As we know from watching men, it is an open question whether we will choose to use unearned advantage, and whether we will use any of our arbitrarily awarded power to try to reconstruct power systems on a broader base.[72]

I have quoted McIntosh's work at length because I believe that it explains the problem of white privilege from the perspective of a white woman who benefits from it. It also explains why self-ordained liberals such as Mrs. Roosevelt are responsible for the sloganeering which has produced the talk of a post-racial America in which whites refuse to acknowledge their privilege rather than demanding that whites "get over racism." In my own experience, the allegedly liberal halls of academe are the paradigmatic example of how white privilege operates out in the open. Liberal white academics, like Mrs. Roosevelt, use their white privilege to oppress people of color. In the academy, they do this by marginalizing the scholarship and research of academics of color by categorizing our work as "ghetto scholarship" and or demanding that we assimilate or be labeled angry, recalcitrant, unproductive or incompetent. In the halls of the liberal academy, hegemonic scholarship has been presented as the ideal, thus, worthy of emulation.

Just as Mrs. Roosevelt was working for civil rights and against human rights because white privilege allowed her to select the kind of acceptable blacks she would consider worthy of her company and advocacy, white privilege allows white liberals in academia to brand as "real scholars" those black academics who defend, rather than challenge, white privilege or who expose the hypocrisy of these liberals in the marketplace of ideas. Black male academics in particular experi-

---

[72] Peggy McIntosh, "White Privilege: Unpacking the Invisible Knapsack," *Peace and Freedom* (Jul./Aug. 1989) Working Paper 189.

ence attempts by both white male and female liberal academics who try to subordinate both our race and masculinity and who fundamentally believe that we should be grateful that they have "allowed" us into their institutions. The result is growing dissatisfaction by an entire generation of black male scholars who find ourselves committed to teaching and research, but having to make a very real choice between challenging white privilege in the academy, thus liberating our race and masculinity, or failing to call out white privilege, thus participating in our own oppression.

This is not, however, simply a matter of individual liberal white academics benefiting from white privilege. First, in my experience, these academics either doubt the existence and impact of white privilege or intellectualize it into oblivion. For example, when an institution has done a "national" search for a leadership position in the academy and they have proclaimed diversity as "open hearts, minds, and doors," what, except white privilege, explains why, at the end of the search, they end up with one candidate for the position and that candidate is a white male?

Second, liberal white academics in my experience internalize their white supremacy and just as Mrs. Roosevelt's best friends were Negro, the academics of whom I speak are proud of the fact that they have changed their party affiliation to vote for Barack Obama and proclaim the value of diversity and ant-racism.

Third, in my experience, liberal white academics are diversity pimps. They package and sell diversity, EEO, and inclusion training and education, and thus profit from this pimping. They believe that they have no attendant responsibility for eradicating racism and white privilege in the academy. The reality is that white privilege has become as much a part of the academy as educational pedagogy. The academics of whom I speak hold the figurative keys to the academy and use those keys to lock black academics in or out.

Fourth, these liberal white academics are often helped along in their practice of white privilege by our own black colleagues, who like the house Negro of old, assure them that our work is substandard. This is because they want to be in the "big house."

Finally, white privilege as both Mrs. Roosevelt and the liberal white academics of whom I speak have demonstrated, encourages white liberals to be post-racial while jumpin' Jim Crow.

CHAPTER SEVEN
THE RED BADGE OF SHAME

While egos, in-fighting, and support from Eleanor Roosevelt all helped contribute to the NAACP's decisions during the 1940s and 1950s to move away from human rights issues and toward civil rights issues, communism and all of its ramifications contributed significantly as well. World War II had ended and the nation had entered into a Cold War. A major problem experienced by America during that time was that the Soviet Union was excoriating it for its race relations problem. With the start of the Cold War, the United States faced immense international pressure to live up to its Cold War rhetoric regarding democratic ideals. President Truman summarized this in 1947: "When we fail to live together in peace, the failure touches not us, as American, alone, but the cause of democracy itself in the whole world. That we must never forget."[73] Truman's comment reflected the importance of a country's image in the international media during the Cold War. The United Soviet Socialist Republic (USSR), America's communist enemy, frequently denounced the United States for its domestic struggle with race relations in an effort to sway the newly independent countries in the Middle East and Africa towards communism.[74]

---

[73] Philip A. Klinkner and Rogers M. Smith, *The Unsteady March* (Chicago: University of Chicago Press, 1999) 213.

[74] "President's Committee on Civil Rights: Truman's Response to the Cold War Battle in the International Media," 10 Mar. 2008 <http://www.piedmontcommunities.us/servlet/go_ProcServ/dbpage=page&gid=0133600115108233325 3641240>.

A byproduct of the Cold War was "red hysteria" and America ensured that it used propaganda as a tool to quash communism. In America, communism was the great scourge and so anyone who was "painted red" was immediately attacked. Despite this, Du Bois made it clear that he supported the views of the communist party without apology. In fact, it was the soviets who had planned to take the issue of the lynchings of blacks to the world stage when the United States complained of human rights violations there.

Walter White was very protective of the NAACP and wanted to make sure that it would not die because of its communist ties. Du Bois made no secret of his socialist views and in fact felt that this attachment to socialism would help advance the cause. The problem, of course, was that Du Bois did not speak for the NAACP. However, as the editor of *The Crisis,* and as the foremost intellectual of the organization, his positions supporting communism were attributed to the NAACP. Du Bois' affiliations with socialist thought and his courting of the Communist Party USA were used as powerful propaganda tools against the NAACP by those who did not support the organization's fight for equality. Communist hysteria provided cover to attack and weaken the NAACP, while the communists in Europe actively courted the membership of the NAACP for conversion. NAACP detractors used the following words of a high-ranking communist official as "proof" of the NAACP's communist leanings. According to this official:

> We must realize that our Party's most powerful weapon is racial tension. By propounding into the consciousness of the dark races, that for centuries have been oppressed by the whites, we can mold them to the program of the Communist Party. [. . .] In America, we will aim for subtle victory. While enflaming the Negro minority against the whites, we will instill in the whites a guilt complex for the exploitation of the Negroes. We will aid the Negroes to rise to prominence in every walk of life, in the professions, and in the world of sports and entertainment. With this prestige, the Negroes will

be able to intermarry with the whites, and begin a process which will deliver America to our cause.[75]

Of course for whites, the thought of blacks conspiring to "breed" their white women and bear nigger babies was tantamount to genocide of the white race. The fact that blacks would be engaged in miscegenation at all, much less at the behest of communists was treasonous. Thus, this hardened racial positions and feelings towards blacks, and further weakened any prospect of black human rights. Blacks were now believed to be not only inhuman, they were also communists and the NAACP was leading the charge.

In 1925, a dozen blacks were recruited for propaganda training in Russia. That same year, the American Negro Labor Congress was established. In 1930, they changed their name to the League of Struggle for Negro Rights. They merged with the United Negro Congress when it was founded in 1936 in Washington, D.C. By 1940, communists made up two-thirds of its membership. In 1947, they united with the Civil Rights Congress, a communist front group.[76] The Russian Comintern provided funds totaling more than $300,000 for the purpose of spreading its message among blacks in America with the hopes that they would be so fed up with fighting the government for their rights that they would come to support a new form of government, communism.[77]

The communist party believed if it could convince the blacks of America that the communist way would provide them with true equality, then blacks would support the movement and develop the party's strength and power from within the nation. In James Cannon's *America's Road to Socialism,* he says that the Negroes:

> will play a great and decisive role in the revolution. [. . .] And why shouldn't they be? They have nothing to lose but their poverty and discrimination, and a whole world of prosperity, freedom, and equality to gain. You can bet your boots the Ne-

---

[75] "Final Warning: A History of the New World Order," *The Modern History Project*, 10 Mar. 2008 <http://www.modernhistoryproject .org/mhp/ArticleDisplay.php?Article=FinalWarn04> par. 1– 4.

[76] "Final Warning: A History of the New World Order."

[77] "Final Warning: A History of the New World Order."

gro will join the Revolution to fight for that—once it becomes clear to them that it cannot be gained except by revolution.[78]

These events and statements convinced America's political leadership that it needed to do something, at least symbolically, to show that it was concerned about civil rights. It was a choice between symbolic civil rights and communism. So, while America did not necessarily want black equality, the social and political reality was that the message of the communist party was starting to resonate with blacks. The danger, of course, was that the alignment of blacks with communism would be an unmanageable situation. The thought of approximately 13 million black communists on American soil was simply too much. Communist party members were infiltrating the ranks of the NAACP by joining to gain trust and encourage loyalty to the communist party. Many people found the following statement by J. Peters, shocking:

> The other important ally of the American proletariat is their mass of 13,000,000 Negro people in their struggle against national oppression. The Communist Party, as the revolutionary party of the proletariat, is the only party which is courageously and resolutely carrying on a struggle against the double exploitation and national oppression of the Negro people, becoming intense with the developing crisis, [and] can win over the great masses of the Negro people as allies of the Proletariat against the American bourgeoisie.[79]

The threat of a massive Negro uprising set the American institutions in motion. Since the courts had been so complicit in the legal subordination of blacks, they were quick to act by issuing political decisions under legal cover.

The United States Supreme Court, under Chief Justice Warren, issued a federal desegregation order in 1954, and Eisenhower and Kennedy enforced it by using Federal troops. This effort was meant to serve notice that the United States would provide desegregation to its Negroes; therefore, there was no need for them to align with the communists. In addition, it was a message to Du Bois that his socialist leanings

---

[78] "Final Warning: A History of the New World Order."

[79] J. Peters, *The Communist Party: A Manual on Organization* (New York City: Workers Library Publishers, Jul. 1935) 10.

were not acceptable. W. E. B. Du Bois was a vociferous supporter of socialist thought. However, the entire NAACP was not. In addition, the communist party had decided it wanted to overthrow the American government from the inside out, using the blacks that it was trying to recruit. The leadership of the NAACP soon began to realize the political fallout should it formally align itself with the communist party. For one thing, the leadership knew that the support it was getting from whites was fragile at best. The leadership knew that it could not align itself with the communist party when the power of the United States government was against it.

> The anticommunist hysteria of the early Cold War put tremendous pressure on the civil rights movement. As a consequence, unity was destroyed and its radical left wing fell victim to the witch-hunts of the red scare, while most black leaders and organizations of the civil rights mainstream joined the camp of Cold War liberalism. The NAACP followed a pattern of accommodation to the anticommunist *Zeitgeist* that was typical for the American public at large. It fervently denied all charges that it was dominated by Communists and distanced itself from all groups and individuals suspected of Communist affiliations. At the same time, it defended racial reform as an integral part of the liberal agenda. The NAACP's embrace of liberal anticommunism provoked criticism at the time and has continued to do so among historians of the black civil rights struggle. Indeed, the controversy over the attitude of the NAACP in the early Cold War mirrors the debate over the historical legitimacy of liberal anticommunism and its consequences for American society.[80]

The leadership had experienced the wrath and power of the United States government. The time had come for the NAACP to take a public stand and distance itself from any perceived affiliation with the communist party so that the American people would not withdraw the tentative support that it has just begun to give to the organization. As quick-

---

[80] Manfred Berg, "Black Civil Rights and Liberal Anticommunism: The NAACP in the Early Cold War," *The Journal of American History* 94.1 (2007): 49 pars., 14 Mar. 2008 <http://www.historycooperative.org/journals/jah/94.1/berg.html> par. 2.

quickly and strongly as the NAACP worked to distance itself from any perception that it was a communist party supporter, detractors of the NAACP worked to align the organization with the communists. Religious and political leaders who were not in favor of desegregation or equality began to speak publicly about their belief that key leaders and friends of the NAACP were communist supporters.

Martin Luther King, who had thrown his support behind the NAACP was accused by several detractors of being a communist or at least sympathetic to the communist cause. Rev. Uriah J. Fields, King's secretary during the early years, wrote about him: "King helps to advance communism. He is surrounded with communists. This is the major reason I severed my relationship with him during the fifties. He is soft on communism."[81] In another incident, an FBI agent testified that when he infiltrated the communist party Martin Luther King was often spoken of as a hero to the communist party.

Not one of these accounts actually provided evidence that the NAACP was a communist supporting group, or that as an organization it was going to help the communist cause in any way. However, for the NAACP, the choice was clear. It had to act forcefully, decisively, and quickly to distance itself from the communist party or face seeing the erasure of the gains it had made. Those who were using communism to discredit the NAACP were insisting to the American public that the human rights violations the NAACP had been concerned with as an organization were actually part of a communist plot.[82] The communists used human rights issues to claim that capitalists were mistreating anyone of a lower economic class. The human rights issues that the NAACP was concerned with were bundled with the communist beliefs by those who wanted to discredit the NAACP and its quest for human rights.

As a practical matter, the NAACP was race-baited and red-baited. Anti-communist forces engaged in spinning the work of the NAACP as the work of communists. They ably used the fear of communism to brand the fight for human rights by blacks as a fight to adopt commu-

[81] "Final Warning: A History of the New World Order."

[82] Wilson Record, *Race and Radicalism: The NAACP and the Communist Party in Conflict* (Cornell University Press, 1964).

nist ideology. Internally, the NAACP was so bloodied by its own internal strife, its own over-reliance on the kindness of white folks, and the seduction of formal equality that it could not summon the courage to respond effectively to race-baiting in the form of red-baiting. The NAACP, as a deeply chastened organization, decided that the fight for black equality would have to be vindicated through domestic courts and legislatures by the same racists who created racism. They had lost the game of chicken.

The NAACP had to do its best to avoid giving the appearance that it embraced the communist cause, so its focus was directed toward rights that were without question American. It wrapped itself in the United States Constitution and its hollow and non-specific promises of equality. The theory was that by doing so it would prove to liberal and sympathetic whites that the NAACP was not aligning itself with the communists. It was during this time that the NAACP took strong legalistic measures to fight for civil rights instead of human rights as was evidenced by *Brown v. Board of Education.*

The *Brown v. Board of Education* litigation was attractive for several reasons. First, Eleanor Roosevelt had already taken up the issue of educational equality. Second, it provided the foundation upon which to fight for the constitutional rights of all blacks by starting with the fact that students who were black were being discriminated against on the basis of race for no cognizable reason. Third, the concept of educational equality was one that would resonate with many liberal whites. Finally, education could not be easily attacked as communist propaganda.

However noble and laudable the decision in *Brown* was, it was not without criticism. Consider this critique by former Harvard Law Professor Derrick Bell:

> I contend that the decision in *Brown* to break with the court's long-held position on these issues cannot be understood without some consideration of the decision's value to whites, not simply those concerned about the immorality of racial inequality, but also those whites in policymaking positions able to see the economic and political advances at home and abroad would follow the abandonment of segregation.

First, the decision helped to provide immediate credibility to America's struggle with communist countries to win the hearts and minds of emerging third world peoples. [...]Second, *Brown* offered much needed reassurance to American blacks that the precepts of equality and freedom so heralded during World War II might yet be given meaning at home.[...]Finally, there were whites who realized that the South could make the transition from a rural plantation society to the sunbelt with all its potential profit only when it ended its struggle to remain divided by state-sponsored segregation. Thus, segregation was viewed as a barrier to further industrialization in the South.[83]

Professor Bell lays bear the internal struggle within the NAACP. On the surface, *Brown* seemed great news. However, it was an attempt to address the issues of white guilt, communism, and false promises. *Brown* was about civil rights. It was not about human rights. The infighting at the NAACP continued in part due to the legalistic strategy that would become the organization's imprimatur. The infighting continued and the human rights agenda was gone.

---

[83] Derrick A. Bell, Jr., "Brown v. Board of Education and the Interest-Convergence Dilemma," *Harvard Law Rev.* 93.3 (Jan. 1980): 524–525.

CHAPTER EIGHT
OF EGOS, INFIGHTING, AND THE NAACP

Given the issues that the NAACP faced, the turbulent times in which it developed, and the very difficult battles it had to fight, it is no wonder that there were egos and infighting to be addressed. However, during the 1940s and 1950s, and in the years leading up to that time, the egos and infighting became so intense and continuous that they detracted from the goals of the organization. While Du Bois was working with the NAACP and promoting its publication, *The Crisis,* others around the world and the nation were also working for the NAACP's goals. One such person was Marcus Garvey.

Garvey was born in St. Ann's Bay, Jamaica on August 17, 1887. His family members were sharecroppers and direct descendants of African slaves. He often said that his relatives were a rebellious lot and in fact were active participants in uprisings against British colonial rule and slavery in the early 19th century. It was perhaps this rebellious streak in Garvey's DNA that gave him such a great sense of pride. While blackness was a sense of shame for others, for him, it was to be celebrated. Garvey was entrenched in politics at an early age and traveled from Jamaica to Costa Rica when he was 23 and "LaNacion" had just been published. It was in this paper that he wrote a stirring editorial demanding the improvement of working conditions for black people. He traveled to London and continued his quest for the improvement of the lives of black people. His quest ultimately took him to America.

Based on his love of black people, the condition of black people worldwide, and his activist political streak, he formed the Universal Negro Improvement and Conservation Association and African Communities (Imperial), the organization would later be known as the Universal Negro Improvement Association. According to Garvey:

> We believe that the black people should have a country of their own where they should be given the fullest opportunity to develop politically, socially and industrially. The black people should not be encouraged to remain in white people's countries and expect to be Presidents, Governors, Mayors, Senators, Congressmen, Judges and social and industrial leaders. We believe that with the rising ambition of the negro, if a country is not provided for him in another 50 or 100 years, there will be a terrible clash that will end disastrously to him and disgrace our civilization. We desire to prevent such a clash by pointing the negro to a home of his own. We feel that all well disposed and broad minded white men will aid in this direction. It is because of this belief no doubt that my negro enemies, so as to prejudice me further in the opinion of the public, wickedly state that I am a member of the Ku Klux Klan, even though I am a black man.[84]

The idea of a so-called black nation did not sit well with many blacks in the upper echelon of Jamaica causing Garvey to quip, "I had to decide whether to please my friends and be one of the 'black whites' of Jamaica, and be reasonably prosperous, or come out openly, and defend and help improve and protect the integrity of the black millions and suffer."[85]

The organization never seemed to attain a sufficient footing in Jamaica. This could have been due to the open and notorious opposition, as well as covert opposition, of the black elite. In any event, Garvey left Jamaica two years after the founding of UNIA and immigrated to the United States on an expansionist mission. Not surprisingly, his arrival and success with encouraging blacks to join his UNIA in significant numbers rankled the NAACP and its supporters. Garvey's oratory and

---

[84] Marcus Garvey, Editorial, *The Negro World*, 13 Feb. 1923.

[85] Garvey.

call for direct action to improve the lives of black people was a powerful message to what many blacks had considered the NAACP's anemic and tepid response to the "Negro problem." Of Garvey, Du Bois wrote:

> Marcus Garvey is, without doubt, the most dangerous enemy of the Negro race in America and in the world. He is either a lunatic or a traitor. [...] The American Negroes have endured this wretch all too long with fine restraint and every effort at cooperation and understanding. But the end has come. Every man who apologizes for or defends Marcus Garvey from this day forth writes himself down as unworthy of countenance of decent Americans. As for Garvey himself, this open ally of the Ku Klux Klan should be locked up or sent home.[86]

Of Du Bois, Garvey wrote:

> It is no wonder that Du Bois seeks the company of white people, because he hates Black as being ugly...Yet this professor, who sees ugliness in being Black, essays to be a leader of the Negro people and has been trying for over fourteen years to deceive them in connection with the National Association for the Advancement of Colored People. Now what does he mean by advancing Colored people if he hates Black so much? In what direction must we expect his advancement? We can conclude in no other way that it is in the direction of losing our Black identity and becoming, as nearly as possible, the lowest Whites by assimilation and miscegenation.[87]

As hard and uncharming as Du Bois could be, Garvey was equally his opposite. He was able to gain the support of the masses and was considered extremely appealing and charming by those who heard him speak. While Du Bois wanted to place the blame for the plight of blacks on whites, Garvey challenged blacks to stand up, make something of their lives, and show the world what they were made of. The battle between the two men was not simply a personal one. It was also a fight for which organization would lead the black people. Du Bois, the NAACP, the government, as well as the media, worked in concert to label Garvey as simply too radical to be a leader. The Lusk Committee

---

[86] W. E. B. Du Bois, Editorial, *The Crisis* (May 1924).

[87] Garvey.

of the New York State Legislature wrote a report entitled "Revolution-ary Radicalism" which took direct aim at Garvey and the UNIA.

> The most interesting features of radical and revolutionary propaganda is the appeal made to those elements of our popu-lation that have a just cause of complaint with the treatment they have received in this country. The very fact that the negro has many just causes of complaint adds to the seriousness of the propaganda, and we should encourage all negroes loyal to us to oppose the activities of such radicals, which cannot but lead to serious trouble if they are permitted to continue the propaganda which they now disseminate in such large vol-umes.

The NAACP would do nothing to oppose the findings and conclusions in the report and sat idly by when Garvey was later convicted of fraud with ethereal evidence and deported.

Garvey was not the only person with whom Du Bois fought. Be-fore he left the NAACP, there were significant internal struggles be-tween him and Booker T. Washington. The following two statements illustrate the philosophical differences between the two men; the first being Du Bois and the second Washington. "We claim for ourselves every single right that belongs to a free American, political, civil and social, and until we get these rights we will never cease to protest and assail the ears of America."[88] "The wisest among my race understand that the agitation of questions of social equality is the extremist folly, and that progress in the enjoyment of all the privileges that will come to us must be the result of severe and constant struggle rather than of arti-ficial forcing."[89] At the time, black liberals were more inclined to side with Du Bois, while black conservatives tended to agree with Washing-ton. These were not simply personality conflicts, they were deeply in-tense struggles that would determine the future of the NAACP, as well as the shape and contours of black rights for years to come.

---

[88] Ellis Washington, "Du Bois vs. Washington: Old Lessons Black People Have Not Learned," 2001, *Issues and Views*, 12 May 2008 <http://www.issues-views.com/index.php/sect/1000/article/999> par. 1.

[89] Washington par. 2.

As an early strategy, the NAACP did in fact take its human rights agenda to the United Nations. There were several historical elements that contributed to the NAACP's decisions during the 1940s and 1950s to move its agenda and spotlight away from human rights and focus on civil rights. The infighting played a part in the unrest that the organization faced, not only internally, but also publicly before the nation. The support of Eleanor Roosevelt while she was the nation's first lady had a significant impact on the direction that the NAACP took during those years. Eleanor Roosevelt was not only a member of the NAACP Board of Directors, she would go on to become chair of the United Nations' Commission on Human Rights once she left the White House. As such, she had significant policy-making authority. On its surface, it would seem that she would have pushed the NAACP's human rights agenda along. As Du Bois and others who supported human rights discovered, this was an unreasonable expectation, since as a former first lady she was also a politician. As Professor Carol Anderson pointed out:

> Eleanor Roosevelt was a key element in stopping the NAACP's petition from being heard by the Commission on Human Rights. And after that petition got scuttled, she then did what I call the education of Walter White, letting him know exactly where the NAACP had erred in exposing the United States to international ridicule for its treatment of its African American population. In fact, in a heated exchange with W. E. B. Du Bois, Roosevelt had said, 'As far as she was concerned, the colored people in the United States would be better served in the long run if the NAACP were not placed on the agenda of the UN.' After she had really berated Walter White for even going that far, taking that step, she then did the ultimate, and that is to resign from the Board of Directors of the NAACP. Walter White looked like a James Brown video, begging her, 'Please, Eleanor, don't go! Please, don't go— your name means so much to us.' And think about that— you've got a powerful, former first lady sitting on your Board of Directors in 1947—that's cachet, that's clout, that's prestige, that gets you into doors that you would never be able to get into before. And so, the NAACP is now having to make some very conscious decisions about does it push Eleanor

Roosevelt so far that they alienate a powerful ally, or do they back off of human rights as the agenda? They chose to back off.[90]

White and others should have had some idea of her true position on the "Negro question" earlier, when she was first lady. In that capacity, she took the race issue to her husband, the President and then wrote to to Walter White "her Negro friend" (see Figure 1). She claims that while she was horrified by lynching, she made it clear that the Constitution, at least according to her husband, forbade the president from doing anything about it. It would be the same type of excuse she would use to scuttle the NAACP's human rights petition at the UN when she asserted that the UN could not act because of the concept of sovereignty.

Given the quest for equality in the United States, the NAACP was in a unique position. It gained membership, it engaged the world on issues of civil and human rights, and it was beginning to amass the infrastructure to sustain change. However, the leaders of the organization, including White and Du Bois became drunk with power, enamored with themselves, and more concerned about upstaging one another than about focusing on the people for whom they were supposed to be fighting. In addition, White was so seduced by the power of Mrs. Roosevelt that he failed to see that she was committed to securing her place in history, power, and politics. In her view, attaining civil rights was an acceptable alternative to human rights, because to push for the later meant that the United States would be embarrassed on the world stage. In her view, as the consummate politician, the protection of the reputation of the United States as a moral superpower was more important than black human rights. In short, they all became bigger than the cause.

---

[90] Dr. Carol Anderson, "Human Rights at Home," keynote address, Women's Foundation of California, San Francisco, California, 11 Jan. 2006.

PERSONAL AND CONFIDENTIAL.

THE WHITE HOUSE
WASHINGTON

March 19, 1936

RTW. 3-21-36

My dear Mr. White:

Before I received your letter today I had been in to the President, talking to him about your letter enclosing that of the Attorney General. I told him that it seemed rather terrible that one could get nothing done and that I did not blame you in the least for feeling there was no interest in this very serious question. I asked him if there were any possibility of getting even one step taken, and he said the difficulty is that it is unconstitutional apparently for the Federal Government to step in in the lynching situation. The Government has only been allowed to do anything about kidnapping because of its interstate aspect, and even that has not as yet been appealed so they are not sure that it will be declared constitutional.

The President feels that lynching is a question of education in the states, rallying good citizens, and creating public opinion so that the localities themselves will wipe it out. However, if it were done by a Northerner, it will have an antagonistic effect. I will talk to him again about the Van Nuys resolution and will try to talk also to Senator Byrnes and get his point of view. I am deeply troubled about the whole situation as it seems to be a terrible thing to stand by and let it continue and feel that one cannot speak out as to his feeling. I think your next step would be to talk to the more prominent members of the Senate.

Very sincerely yours,

Eleanor Roosevelt

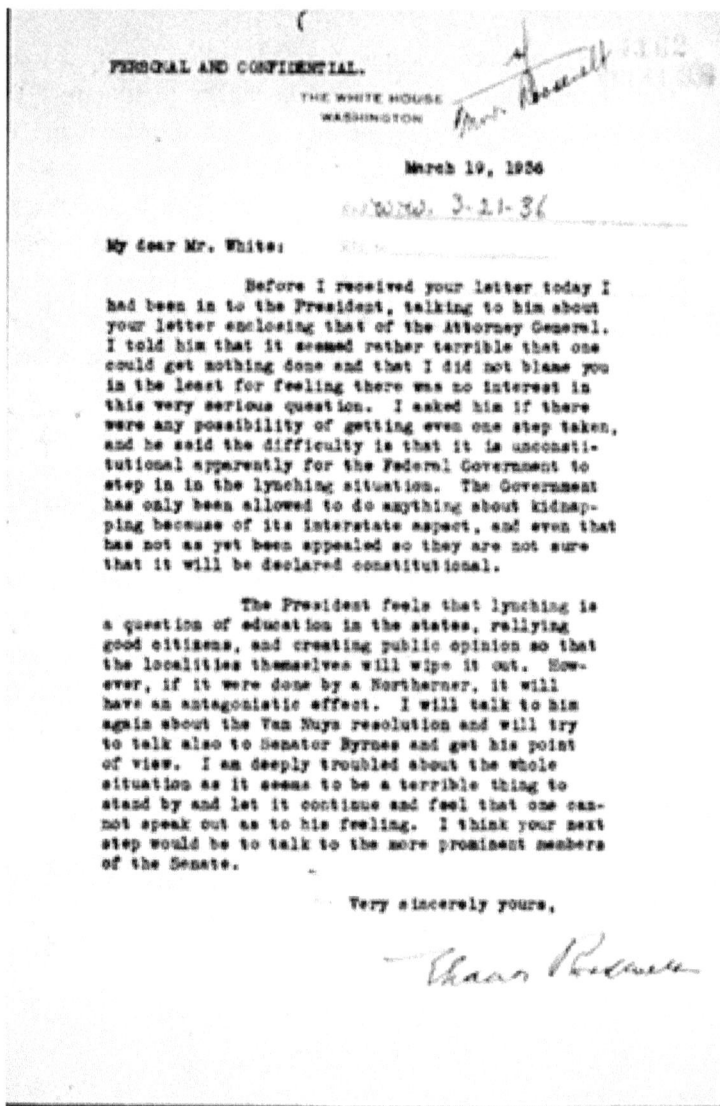

Figure 1: Letter from Eleanor Roosevelt to Walter White.

Du Bois, though brilliant, was too impressed with his own intellect to see that the cause was bigger than he was. He took the position that the quest for human rights would not and could not move forward if he was not front and center. He did not believe that he needed to compromise, because he believed his own press. Du Bois had an unprecedented opportunity to push his human rights agenda working with White. However, Du Bois chose not to compromise his beliefs for the good of the larger cause. Professor Anderson puts its best:

> The chances for African-American equality, given the endemic racism in the United States, were never very great; but those chances dwindled significantly when the black leadership relentlessly attacked each other. What White and Du Bois failed to realize was that it was not a question of either/or; it was a question of both. The struggle for African-American' human rights required the NAACP's petition and a strong Declaration and Covenant on Human Rights. Du Bois was right on target. *An Appeal to the World* was an omnipresent force that compelled the United States to maneuver and counter maneuver against consistent international 'criticism against the treatment of the negroes.' Legal historian Mary Dudziak, in fact, has documented how essential international pressure was in getting the Truman administration to support several desegregation lawsuits. Yet, those cases shaved the outer layers of a glacier that had frozen African-Americans out of the political and economic mainstream of America for centuries.[91]

While there is no doubt that racism is not as overt as it once was, it is still present in American society. Despite all of its social accomplishments and laudatory civil rights victories, the NAACP is first and foremost a political organization. Thus, its decision to choose civil rights (the path of least resistance) must be analyzed in political terms. The NAACP has worked hard to gain civil rights for blacks and has been successful in many areas of the government and private sector. The critique is not that the civil rights strategy was a failure. It is instead that the NAACP chose to sacrifice its human rights strategy and adopted a civil rights strategy. This decision is largely responsible for

---

[91] Anderson, *Eyes off the Prize,* 150.

the dismal economic conditions that continue to beset blacks in America today.

While the NAACP began as a human rights and civil rights organization, it made decisions in the 1940s that served to move its focus to civil rights and away from human rights. It decided to take Mrs. Roosevelt at her word, chose to believe that she was "the ultimate friend of the Negro," and did not challenge her political machinations. These were fatal decisions. In addition, the NAACP felt the need to distance itself from the communist party and made the decision to do so with a strong focus on civil rights, which are singularly protected by the United States Constitution. Finally, the infighting and ego issues within the NAACP contributed to the decision to move toward civil rights and away from human rights issues.

The change in focus was accomplished by providing directed, structured legal avenues to civil rights, as established in the case of *Brown v. the Board of Education.* This decision provided a backdrop for a legal approach to human rights issues and a reliance on the fairness, neutrality, and impartiality of the American legal system. The problem, of course, was that the United States legal system was as political as any other system in government, and continues to be today. For evidence of this we look to the politically charged decisions made by the United States Supreme Court in the most recent Affirmative Action cases of *Gratz* and *Grutter,* which limited the application of Affirmative Action in college admissions. These decisions illustrate that a civil rights strategy is a deeply flawed approach to gaining true equality in a post-slavery world.

First, these decisions show that civil rights are limited in what they can provide in terms of compensation for the lingering effects of slavery. Second, these decisions demonstrate that courts are free to give, curtail, or take away civil rights with a single opinion. Finally, these decisions demonstrate that the NAACP's abandonment of a human rights strategy, though politically expedient, was short sighted. Imagine if the NAACP had pursued a civil rights strategy in the American court system while also fighting for the option to bring the United States to the United Nations for deprivation of economic rights, as well as other rights, under the Universal Declaration of Human Rights.

The NAACP cannot deny its responsibility for the current state of blacks in America. It was charged with the advancement of blacks in America and it failed because White, Du Bois, and Roosevelt put their interests above those of the people for whom they were supposed to serve as advocate. The NAACP did not understand the political currency of communism, choosing instead to be red-baited. It settled for civil rights without critically evaluating the durability of human rights. In so doing, it sent the message that blacks were not entitled to universal human rights and that they should be given the rights that their former oppressors chose to give them and in the increments they deemed sufficient. The civil rights legalistic approach was too tactical, thus less substantive. Finally, the NAACP began with the best of intentions, and ended up with little more than mediocre results. So, how did the NAACP get it so wrong on human rights? What did it miss?

For all of its success, human rights and international law were still contested concepts and realities that would continue to be debated and discussed, and the inherently political nature of the discourse of collective rights, in particular, held much more promise for substantive rights for blacks than civil rights. America was emerging as a loose confederation of nation-states in which human rights would be defined, debated, and enforced under a rubric largely organized in the post-World War II era. The instrument that would help the states define human rights was the Universal Declaration of Human Rights. "On the whole the Declaration remains a lodestar, which has guided the community of States as they gradually emerged from the dark age when the possession of armies, guns and warships was the sole factor for judging the conduct of States, and there were no generally accepted principles for distinguishing good from evil in the world community."[92] Moreover, the rights discourse is consistently shifting from Westerncentric to culturally influenced, as a result of the growing diversity of the world, as well as the advocacy for culturally conscious rights, which is being driven at least in part by the previously subordinated people who want to ensure that they retain some authority to define rights in a post-colonial society as the contours of rights discourse continue to evolve.

---

[92] Antonio Cassese, *International Law* (New York: Oxford University Press, 2005) 382.

As a result of the evolving human rights discourse, or perhaps in spite of it, the individual, as well as the collective nature of human rights will continue to be explored with increasing interest and fervor. As constructed and understood, human rights laws, specifically as enunciated by the Universal Declaration of Human Rights, are based on the rights of the individual. "The Universal Declaration of Human Rights is based on the assumption that individual human rights, including the prohibition of discrimination and the right to practice one's culture, are sufficient to protect cultural minorities."[93] This is the liberal notion of the rights of the individual and the need to protect those rights, and thus the individual, from abuses by the state. Given the cultural context of rights, it is possible that collectives can have rights.

The developing human rights framework allows, much to America's chagrin, for the recognition and protection of collective rights independent of enforcement mechanisms. There is room for both individual and collective rights in human rights law, and there is a need to examine how individual and collective rights can co-exist and whether there can be mechanisms that will enforce individual rights while leaving open the space for collective rights. Collective rights have not attained the status and acceptance of individual rights, and in fact, some argue that collective rights are inconsistent with individual rights.[94] These arguments should not be dismissed uncritically. However, since human rights laws and norms are evolving and the work of human rights is incomplete, characterizing human rights as 'essentially' individualistic is a starting point for analysis; it is not the ending point.

THE UDHR AND ITS INDIVIDUALISTIC UNDERPINNINGS

The Universal Declaration of Human Rights was adopted by the United Nations in 1947. Member states signed onto the 30 articles.

---

[93] Michael Freeman, *Human Rights: An Interdisciplinary Approach* (Hoboken, New Jersey: Wiley & Sons, Inc., 2002) 114.

[94] Sakah S. Mahmud, The State and Human Rights in Africa in the 1990s: Perspectives and Prospects, *Hum. Rts. Q.* 15 (1993): 485-98. [Revision of paper delivered at the Conference on Africa and Global Human Rights, which argues that the concept of collective rights is used by many African countries as a method of violating, rather than protecting human rights.]

Rather than give people rights, it states what human rights are in a grand vision of humanity. In 1966, the general assembly adopted the two detailed covenants which complete the International Bill of Human Rights; and in 1976, after the covenants had been ratified by a sufficient number of individual nations, the bill soon became normative international law.[95] The UDHR has the following components:

- All human beings are born free and equal in dignity and rights.[96]
- Right to life, liberty and security of person.[97]
- Right to recognition everywhere as a person before the law and are entitled without any discrimination to equal protection of the law.[98]
- No one should be in slavery or servitude.[99]
- No one should be subjected to arbitrary arrest, detention or exile.[100]
- Right to be presumed innocent until proven guilty at a public trial.[101]
- No one shall be arbitrarily deprived of property.[102]
- Freedom of thought, conscience and religion.[103]

---

[95] Paul Williams, ed., *The International Bill of Human Rights* (Glen Ellen, CA: Entwhistle Books, 1981).

[96] United Nations, "Universal Declaration of Human Rights," Jan. 1997, *Human Rights Web*, 8 Mar. 2008 <www.hrweb.org/legal/ udhr.html> Article 1.

[97] United Nations Article 3.

[98] United Nations Articles 6–7.

[99] United Nations Article 4.

[100] United Nations Article 9.

[101] United Nations Article 11.

[102] United Nations Article 17, par. 2.

[103] United Nations Article 18.

- Freedom of opinion, expression and assembly.[104]

As written, the UDHR sought to protect the individual from abuses by the state. As a strictly legal matter, while the declaration declared these rights, regional instruments codified them into legally binding agreements, thus ensuring their durability and enforceability. It is important to contextualize how individuals were defined. "The political theory of liberal democracy was not designed to solve the problems of cultural minorities. The classic conception of democracy entailed the rule of a culturally unified people. In the influential theory of the eighteenth century French philosopher Rousseau theorized that any cultural differences that might exist in society should be subordinated to the general will of the people."[105]

Given the individual underpinnings of the UDHR, how can it be argued that it foresaw or at least allows for collective rights? First, the plain language of the declaration offers some clues. "Everyone as a member of society has a right to social security."[106] Whereas other language in the UDHR spoke to individual rights, the introduction of "as a member of society" seems to allow for collective inclusion. Second, this concept of the collective suggests that social security is envisioned as a collective right and not exclusively an individual right; it can thus be argued that the UDHR did not, at a minimum, forestall the creation and thus protection of collective rights. Finally, human rights laws and concepts are not static. While the UDHR has remained constant, there have been and continue to be new treaties and documents that illuminate the concepts that have been laid down in the UDHR. This clarification has been, at least in part, due to the changing nature of the world and its racial, ethnic, and other diversity.

Among the clarifying documents on the evolving collective nature of rights are the *International Covenant on Economic, Social and Cultural Rights,* as well as the *Constitution of the International Labour Organization* and the *ILO Convention on Indigenous and Tribal Peoples*. While I understand the intellectual currency of the terms "second

---

[104] United Nations Articles 19–20.

[105] Freeman 115.

[106] United Nations Article 22.

and third generation rights," I reject that currency as privileging one set of rights over another and discuss individual and collective rights without the second-third binary construction.

The spirit of the UDHR, despite its individualistic genesis, is the recognition and protection of rights. The reality is that in many parts of the globe collectives exist, and these collectives in their representational capacity are slowly coming under the ambit of human rights protections. Blacks as a group were the ultimate collective and the NAACP missed this point much to its chagrin. The result was the acceptance of a patchwork of ill defined civil rights that ebb and flow with the pronouncements of an increasingly political American judiciary. The question now turns to collectives and how such collectives merit human rights protections.

COLLECTIVE RIGHTS

Collective rights are those rights that deal with the protection of minorities, as well as with the preservation of non-dominant culture. It is critical to make a distinction between collective rights and rights that are exercised in association with others. Collective rights are based on intergroup solidarities[107] that are central to effective collective action and are thus entrusted to a collective and can only be claimed by those groups or a duly authorized member of said group acting in his or her authorized capacity to claim rights on behalf of the group.[108] They are neither temporal nor transitory and are inextricably linked to the survival of the group's culture. Contrast this with rights that are exercised in association with others. In the latter, for example, a loose collection

---

[107] United Nations Article 27, ICCPR: "In those states in which ethnic, religious or linguistic minorities exist, persons belonging to such minorities shall not be denied the right, in community with the other members of their group, to enjoy their own culture, to profess and practice their own religion, or to use their own language."

[108] Allen E. Buchanan, *Secession: The Morality of Political Divorce from Fort Sumter to Lithuania and Quebec* (Boulder Colorado: Westview Press, 1990): 27–85; Allen E. Buchanan, "The Right to Self-Determination: Analytical and Moral Foundations," *Ariz. J. Int'l & Comp. L.* 8 (1991): 41, 48; Allen E. Buchanan, "Federalism, Secession, and the Morality of Inclusion," *Ariz. L. Rev.* 37 (1995): 53, 54.

of members of a particular ethnic or religious group may organize to gain access to a benefit, but their failure to gain access to that benefit does not mean that the cultural collective will be harmed in its continued existence or functioning. The aforementioned actions are akin to lobbying for a more favorable result in treatment. The failure of such lobbying may affect individual minorities. It will not, however, impact culture or the survival of the minority collective.

The question of collective rights ultimately turns on how the collective is organized. It must be apparent when the collective is speaking whether or not the granting of rights advocated for by the collective results in the violation of minimum human rights standards and how issues of conflict between the rights of individual members and the collective as a whole are resolved. Jovanovic suggests an inherent dilemma in collective rights analysis.

> The concept of minority protection can become fully operational only by transcending the still dominant framework of individual rights and adopting the framework of collective rights; however comprehending collectives as legal rights holders within the current legal theoretical framework protecting collective moral goods without abandoning the language of individual rights, remains a challenge.[109]

Collectives should be set up by the minorities in question to ensure that their voices and interests are protected. In so doing, members of the collective should not simply resort to a 'democratic' process without first understanding that the mere existence of a collective is both a reminder and a warning of the vulnerability of minority rights and of the willingness, in some cases, of others inside and outside the collective to sacrifice and subvert minority rights in furtherance of political and economic ends.

Thus, a collective must be organized with regard to these seldom acknowledged truths or ignore them at its peril. The rules of engagement cannot be rules that serve a covert purpose, as they will never vindicate the rights the collective is ostensibly seeking to protect. It is critical that collectives take as a given that they are not the final authority on what rights are worthy of protection; they must engage the mem-

---

[109] M. Jovanovic, "Recognizing Minority Identities through Collective Rights," *Human Rights Quarterly* 27 (2005): 638.

bers of the collective in a substantive way. Collective rights should begin with an agreement that rights in a collective sense are not fixed and monolithic; they are instead fluctuating, decentralized, and complex; they develop based on relationships, histories, and experiences that are shaped and adjusted under the constant pressures of political events and relationships in and outside collectives.

The challenge in understanding collective rights is to recognize that regardless of "tradition" there are certain fundamental human rights that simply cannot be negotiated away, even if it is being done for the collective good. Moreover, as with analyzing the contours of all rights, there are no absolutes. Collective rights must be defined through an examination of the roles individual identities and needs play in the larger collective rights struggle, while not recreating the same hegemonic structure and subordination that collectives are theoretically organized to dismantle. Addressing collective rights and their inherent conflict with individual rights involves both dismantling the current individualistic focus in rights discourse and challenging the universality of the individual as the exclusive holder of rights in a formal and legalistic paradigm.

The formalistic, individualistic paradigm adhered to uncritically binds individuals and collectives, and normatively directs, controls, regulates, appropriates, and approaches rights in a way that derisively ignores the existence and importance of collectives in the cultural context of rights discourse, application, and protection. The task is to unpack the values and norms of individuals and collectives; however, this has been hindered by the fact that the nomenclature of rights has been developed based on a lexicon of individualistic rights, which have been enshrined in human rights law. Thus, collective rights must be steeped in culture, as defined by John Brenkman for whom culture is seen as constituting the forms of symbolization, representation, and expression through which a group secures its identity and solidarity. Culture enables a group to establish reciprocal relationships and mutual understandings while simultaneously differentiating itself from other groups with which it is interdependently linked, whether as a matter of cooperation or antagonism.[110]

---

[110] J. Brenkman, *Culture and Domination* (Ithaca: Cornell Univ. Press, 1987).

The NAACP was so rocked by internal turmoil that its leadership was unable to develop a vision of collective rights for blacks that would withstand the test of time. Their quest for rights through gratification was a serious tactical mistake that blacks are still paying for in 2008.

CHAPTER NINE
THE AMERICAN CONSTRUCTION OF HETERONORMATIVE MASCULINITY

There is no question that the fight for racial equality took a toll on all blacks in America. Since this edition cannot examine how it affected all blacks, I have chosen for illustrative purposes to discuss the toll on black men. Black men were separated from their families, lynched, and emasculated.

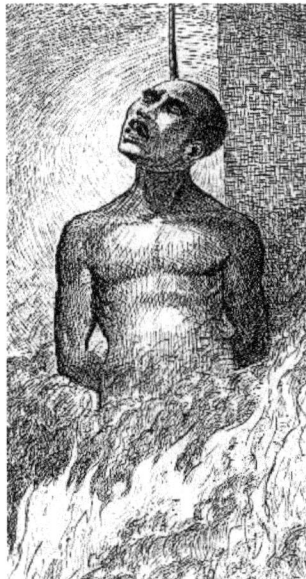

Figure 2: **Source:** *Daily Times-Courier*, **October 26 and 27.**

A member of the lynching party described the lynching in all of its ghastliness, down to the most minute detail:

> After taking the nigger to the woods about four miles from Greenwood, they cut off his penis. He was made to eat it. They cut off his testicles and made him eat them and say he liked it. [. . .] Then they sliced his sides and stomach with knives and every now and then somebody would cut off a finger or toe. Red hot irons were used on the nigger to burn him from top to bottom. From time to time during the torture a rope was tied around Neal's neck and he was pulled up over a limb and held there until he almost choked to death. Then he was let down and the torture began all over again. After several hours of this unspeakable torture, they decided just to kill him.
>
> Neal's body was tied to a rope on the rear of an automobile and dragged over the highway to the Cannidy home. Here a mob estimated to number somewhere between 3000 and 7000 people from eleven southern states was excitedly waiting his arrival. When the car which was dragging Neal's body came in front of the Cannidy home, a man who was riding the rear bumper cut the rope.
>
> A woman came out of the Cannidy house and drove a butcher knife into his heart. Then the crowd came by and some kicked him and some drove their cars over him
>
> Men, women, and children were numbered in the vast throng that came to witness the lynching. It is reported from reliable sources that the little children, some of them mere tots, who lived in the Greenwood neighborhood, waited with sharpened sticks for the return of Neal's body and that when it rolled in the dust on the road that awful night these little children drove their weapons deep into the flesh of the dead man.[111]

A casualty of the abandonment of human rights was the development of a further contested space of masculinity. White men epitomized masculinity, and thus superiority in America. Black men, there-

---

[111] Walter White, "A Report from Walter White on the Lynching of Claude Neal," *ChickenBones: A Journal for Literary & Artistic African-American Themes*, 10 May 2008 <http://www.nathanielturner.com/lynchingclaudeneal.htm>.

fore, had to be constructed as inferior. As America interacted with the rest of the world, it would not only spread its western view of the world, it would also export the white man superiority-black man inferiority binary.

Masculinity and the integral role it plays in America, and as it has been exported to the rest of the world, can be viewed in a number of ways. Among them is the view that masculinity exists in relationship to gender and that masculinity affects men, women, and a man's interaction with other men. "Some images of gender—in particular, hegemonic masculinity and emphasized femininity—predominate over others. Hegemonic masculinity is most closely associated with the ideal mode of conduct for elite, white men in Western capitalist society. It is based on authority, aggressiveness, technical competence, and heterosexist desire for and domination over women."[112]

"The myth of masculinity is to pass itself off as something natural and universal, free of problems."[113] As a consequence, gendered politics are made invisible. For instance, men rarely see themselves as a gender, and society generally treats masculine characteristics as the prototype of human behavior, irrespective of time and space. Masculinity therefore, has traditionally operated as a hegemonic ideology and exerts a profound influence on the structure of development. As Dolan argues,

> [t]his model rests on polarized stereotypes and models of what men and women are like, what they should do, how they should relate to each other, and what their respective positions and roles in society should be. At its simplest it can be described as based on sexist, heterosexist, ethnocentric and adultist premises and entailing considerable economic responsibilities and a particular relationship with the state.[114]

---

[112] Robert Connell, "Masculinities and Globalization," *Men's Lives*, eds. M. S. Kimmel and M. A. Messner (Meedham Heights: Allyn and Bacon, 2000) 615.

[113] Jonathan Rutherford. "Who's That Man?" *Male Order: Unwrapping Masculinity*, eds. R. Chapman and J. Rutherford (London: Lawrence and Wishet, 1988) 23.

[114] C. Dolan, "Collapsing Masculinities and Weak States: A Case Study From Northern Uganda," *Masculinities Matter! Men, Gender and Development*, ed. F. Cleaver (London & New York: Zed Books, 2002) 59.

This edition invites readers to think about masculinity and the fact that it is a core philosophy embedded in white male supremacy and patriarchy. Globalization has not only resulted in exporting gendered institutions, it has also exported American hegemonic masculinity.

This construction of racial boundaries through gender also had a sexual component. White southerners differentiated themselves from 'savages' by attributing to the latter a sexual nature that was more sensual, aggressive, and beastlike than that of whites. Influenced by the Elizabethan image of 'the lusty Moor,' white southerners embraced the notion that blacks were 'lewd, lascivious, and wanton people.'[115] Both their gender similarity and animalized sexuality, white supremacist discourse declared, 'proved' blacks were a subordinate species; therefore, it was natural that races must not mix and that whites must dominate blacks. The ideas of race corporeality defined inequality between whites and blacks and constructed what Frankenberg labels an 'essentialist racist discourse.' Such a discourse constructs blacks as 'fundamentally other than white people: different, inferior, less civilized, less human, more animal, than whites'[116]. The articulation and deployment of essentialist racism as the dominant discourse for thinking about race marks the moment when race is constructed as *difference*: alleged white biological superiority justifies economic, political, and social inequalities in slavery.[117]

---

[115] J. D'Emilio and E.B. Freedman, *Intimate Matters: A History of Sexuality in America* (New York: Harper and Row, 1988) 35.

[116] R. Frankenberg, *White Women, Race Matters: The Social Construction of Whiteness* (Minneapolis: University of Minnesota Press, 1993) 61.

[117] James W. Messerschmidt, "We Must Protect Our Southern Women: On Whiteness, Masculinities, and Lynching," *Race, Gender, and Punishment: From Colonialism to the War on Terror*, eds. M. Bosworth and J. Flavin (New Brunswick, NJ: Rutgers University Press, 2006) 77–94.

PERFORMING MASCULINITY:
BLACK, RED, BROWN, AND WHITE ALL OVER

"It has become almost axiomatic that gender is inextricably implicated in the development process. 'Human development, if not gendered, is endangered' was a central message of the 1995 Human Development Report."[118] Masculinity is a gender ideology that is socially constructed. Therefore, it cannot be said to be static or immutable, but shaped in the context of history and culture. It is important to make a clear distinction between being male and being masculine, because the values of the former may not correspond to the personality or preferences of some biological men (for example, feminized masculinities), while this may be the case for some women (masculinized femininities).

> In analyzing the role of masculinity in provoking or perpetuating violence and conflict in northern Uganda, it is necessary to distinguish between men's lived experiences of their own masculinities, which are necessarily multiple, and their lived expectations of masculinity, which are contained in a hegemonic normative model or set of ideas concerning what defines a man.[119]

The "ideal" male in modern, globalized society has the following characteristics: white, heterosexual, married, middle aged, university educated, and upper middle class. This is the hegemonic conception of Western masculinity by which all men, irrespective of age, class, sexual orientation, or cultural background, are measured. Here, the white male is constructed to be an ideal for others to emulate. The incongruity of course is that the hegemonic ideal male is a mythic construction that few can attain. While black men were part of American society, they are incapable of attaining the storied white male status as they have been constructed to be savages and brutes. The point is that the white male is used as a metaphor for hegemonic masculinity, but it is not exclusive, because in cultural contexts, the ideal can be of a darker hue.

---

[118] Michael Kimmel, foreward, *Masculinities Matter! Men, Gender and Development,* ed. F. Cleaver (London & New York: Zed Books, 2002).

[119] Dolan 60.

Consider masculinity in the context of India, where most of the population is not white:

>This mimicry of a 'western' masculinism, however, is not just mimicry of the colonial structuring of power in gendered terms. It is also a replication of the colonial intent (perhaps inevitably) as if, postcolonially, the only way to possess (to claim or reclaim) an identity was through a second 'colonizing' move.[120]

>In addition to being based on a white male supremacist philosophy, hegemonic masculinity also is based on an inherently heterosexual one. That is, heterosexual is both superior and normal; homosexuality is both inferior and abnormal. The disgust and contempt to homosexuality in hegemonic masculinity offers some insight into gender politics. Homosexuality is generally seen as the rejection of masculinity and thus the embracing of femininity. Homosexual men are often described as the utmost of emasculated men. It is suggested that homophobic responses to gay men are one of the means by which hegemonic masculinity polices the boundaries of a traditional male sex role and reinforces a strict heterosexual practice.[121]

Connell also argues that

>these plural masculinities exist in definite social relations, often relations of hierarchy and exclusion. This was recognized early, in gay theorists' discussions of homophobia; it has become clear that the implications are far-reaching. There is generally a hegemonic form of masculinity, the most honored or desired in a particular context.[122]

Homophobia therefore is one of the key building blocks in the construction of hegemonic masculinity. In the context of the United States' construction of masculinity, black males must be both heterosexual and white to fit the hegemonic masculinity model. The reality is that this

---

[120] Prem Vijayan, "Nationalism and the Developmental State: Exploring Hindutuva Masculinities," *Masculinities Matter! Men, Gender and Development,* ed. F. Cleaver (London & New York: Zed Books, 2002) 28.

[121] Connell 4.

[122] Connell 6.

model is simply unattainable for any black man in the United States post-slavery. However, this is the model that has been largely exported around the globe.

EXPORTING HEGEMONIC MASCULINITY: ACTIONS, REACTIONS, AND CONSEQUENCES

The above description of hegemonic masculinity suggests that the white male hegemonic model requires the marginalization of subordinate masculinities for its survival. Moore suggests that hegemonic masculinity can also play a role in creating and perpetuating violent conflict such as in northern Uganda. She explains:

> There is much to suggest a link between feelings such as humiliation, resentment, oppression, frustration and the use of violence. Moore uses the term 'thwarting' for this dynamic; 'thwarting can be understood as the inability to sustain or properly take up a gendered subject position, resulting in a crisis, real or imagined, or self-representation and/or social evaluation. [...] Thwarting can also be the result of contradictions arising from the taking up of multiple subject positions, and the pressure of multiple expectations about self-identity or social presentation.[123]

Dolan presents mob justice, suicide, male rape, a violent dispute over bride wealth, and suicide due to the humiliation of lacking control over wife, as examples of the effect of the hegemonic masculinity model in developing countries. His examples suggest that this exported hegemonic masculinity model has resulted not only in violence against others, but violence against self when one's masculinity is threatened and or questioned. According to Dolan, there is a very clear link between frustrated expectations and outcomes in all of the examples.

> These examples suggest that the disjuncture between expectations and the ability to live up to them go hand in hand with widespread feelings of fear, intimidation, humiliation, frustration and anger, often expressed in violence against the self and others, in the forms of alcohol abuse, suicide attempts and domestic violence, and also in conflict between civilians and the

---

[123] Henrietta L. Moore, *A Passion for Difference: Essays in Anthropology and Gender* (Cambridge: Polity Press, 1994) 66.

military. They also demonstrate a resort to psychological violence in the form of seeking to oppress powerful individuals, notably youth and women.[124]

In the context of black men and masculinity, Mosher and Sirkin suggest that a hyper-masculine, macho personality was identifiable along three characteristics: (1) a view of violence as manly, (2) a perception of danger as exciting, and (3) callousness toward women.[125] Traditionally, exaggerated masculinity has largely been viewed as a countercultural phenomenon endemic to black and Latino males. This "black and brown" version of manhood has interchangeably been described in the literature as machismo, bravado, macho personality, and hyper-masculinity. Some researchers have suggested that hyper-masculine behavior is a function of race and culture.[126]

> Given the primary objectives of these studies to explain white masculinity as the dominating cultural discourse, it is understandable that black manhood identified frequently gets thinned out to the extreme polar cases of hyper masculinity (as black men's over identification with the white masculine norm or metaphorical emasculation (as black men's total abjection from that norm). For certain, both of these extremes help explain the cultural history of black manhood, but neither successfully adjudicates the complex maneuvering entailed in the ever changing project of black manhood reform as historically situated through enslavement, Jim Crow, Civil Rights, Black Power and other political-cultural movements.[127]

---

[124] Dolan 12.

[125] D. L. Mosher and M. Sirkin, "Measuring a Macho Personality Constellation," *Journal of Research and Personality 18* (1984): 150–163.

[126] Patrick Moynihan, "The Negro Family: The Case for National Action," otherwise known as the Moynihan Report (Washington, D.C.: U.S. Department of Labor, 1965); D. D'Souza, *The End of Racism: Principles for a Multiracial Society* (New York: Free Press, 1995).

[127] Marlon B. Ross, *Manning the Race: Reforming Black Men in the Jim Crow Era* (New York: New York UP, 2004) 7.

Masculinity then is contested and a historically contextualized human quality. Any discussion of race and racism, as well as the human rights of the black man, cannot be understood and analyzed without first understanding the intersection between gender and race in the life of black men. While this edition discusses black men in America, it is critical to understand that men of color in all countries are both raced and gendered. The fact is that masculinity and its post-colonial effects cannot be ignored. George Lipsitz captures the point with sobering clarity.

> Yet whiteness never works in isolation; it functions as part of a broader dynamic grid created through intersections of race, gender class and sexuality. The way these identities work in concert gives them their true social meaning. The renewal of patriotic rhetoric and display in the United States during and after the Reagan presidency serves as the quintessential example of this intersecting operation. Reagan succeeded in fusing the possessive investment in whiteness with other physical and material investment—especially in masculinity, patriarchy and heterosexuality. The intersecting identity he offered gave new meaning to white male patriarchal and heterosexual identities by establishing patriotism as the site where class antagonisms between men could be reconciled in national and patriotic antagonism against foreign foes and internal enemies. By encoding the possessive investment in whiteness within national narratives of male heroism and patriarchal protections, Regan and his allies mobilized a cross class coalition around the premise that the declines in life chances in the United States, the stagnation of real wages, the decline of basic services and infrastructure resources, and the increasing social disintegration stemmed not from the policies of big corporations and their neoliberal and neoconservative allies in government but from harm done to the nation by the civil rights, antiwar, feminist and gay liberation movements of the 1960s and 1970s. By representing the national crisis as a crisis of declining value of white male and heterosexual identity, Regan and his allies and successor built a countersubersive coalition mobilized around protecting the privileges and prerogatives of the possessive in-

vestment in whiteness, in masculinity, in patriarchy, and in heterosexuality.[128]

MASCULINITY, PATRIARCHY, AND RELATIONSHIP

The archetypical patriarch is the dominant father or powerful man who rules over the household or community—including women, younger men, sons, daughters, and slaves. The hegemonic masculinity model is embedded in the subconscious of developing countries. According to Vijayan,

> [It] is in all of them indicative of a general condition of the dominance of men—essentially over women, but also over other oppressed men, the old, the very young, the infirm, and through whatever cross-sections of caste, class or race obtained. It consequently remains a dominance of the masculine, in whatever is the currently dominant, specific form of hegemonic masculinity.[129]

Vijayan seems to be suggesting that representations of hegemonic masculinity, subordinate masculinity, and patriarchy work hand-in-hand to perpetuate the status quo regardless of the cultural context. By status quo, I mean the hegemonic model of masculinity that has been exported by way of globalization or experienced as a result of colonialism. As Connell observes,

> [c]ertainly the process of conquest could produce frontier masculinities that combined the occupational culture of these groups with an unusual level of violence and egocentric individualism. The vehement contemporary debate about the genocidal violence of the Spanish conquistadors—who in fifty years completely exterminated the population of Hispaniola points to this pattern.[130]

---

[128] George Lipsitz, *The Possessive Investment in Whiteness: How White People Profit From Identity Politics* (Philadelphia: Temple UP, 1998) 72.

[129] Vijayan 23.

[130] Connell 7.

The model of hegemonic masculinity requires deconstruction by black men as a collective. In many respects, the work of deconstructing these models has been done by feminists and in some cases, by gay men. While their analyses have been helpful, heterosexual men are also burdened and affected by the model, thus heterosexual men from academia, practice, industry, and all areas of life must also become involved in the deconstruction. The difficulty, however, is that heterosexual men enjoy the privilege of pretending that gender is a women's issue exclusively and that there is no need to deconstruct a model that has no effect on them. The result is deconstruction and analyses that while helpful, have the potential to create a new model of masculinity that may not include the voices of many of those who need to be involved.[131] Their involvement must be at a level at which they understand masculinity is not simply an issue of self-image or an issue about relationships between men and women. They must understand that it is an issue that also involves relationships between men and subordinated masculinities.

BLACK MASCULINITY AND THE CIVIL RIGHTS MOVEMENT

In America, slavery and its aftermath seemed to have permanently subordinated black male masculinity. The civil rights movement held the promise of liberating those subordinated masculinities in that it provided black men with the ability to regain their dignity. That dignity had been taken away from them in part by a social custom that allowed white people to call them "boy," regardless of their age or position. The movement's leaders had hoped that by fighting for equality of opportunity, black male masculinity would be liberated. However, legislation and movement, no matter how fervent, could not easily liberate subordinated masculinity. Slavery, Jim Crow, and racism had conflated black

---

[131] This is not to suggest that there are no heterosexual men involved in this work. It is also not to suggest that men's groups and men's movements do not exist. The examination of such groups and their work is beyond the scope of this edition. It is simply to suggest that the bulk of the work in this area has been done largely by feminist and or gay scholars. This should not be taken as a pejorative; it is simply an argument for a more inclusive approach.

male masculinity with sexuality. Thus, for whites and some blacks, black male masculinity and sexuality were one in the same.

Given the conflation of sexuality and masculinity, black men would be not men, but sex fiends. Prior to the civil rights movement, black men would be lynched for simply looking at a white woman. This was the power of subordinated masculinity. Many whites saw the movement as robbing them of that power. In fact, many whites were simply horrified that the civil rights era gave black men the freedom to sleep with white women and to procreate. The civil rights movement, it seemed, was responsible for defiling the "southern belle." The hard work, the struggle, and the deaths at the hands of whites all culminated in blacks moving closer to "the promised land." However, it was not only whites who would conflate black masculinity and black male sexuality. Prior to the movement, whites handed black men their penises through lynching. After the civil rights movement, many black men would now choose to demonstrate their masculinity by literally and metaphorically grabbing their own penises and holding them as the ultimate sign of black manhood.

Perhaps I expected the movement to deal not only with outward manifestations of hate; but also with the inward manifestation of self-hate. Internalized oppression is the process by which many blacks view images put forth by whites and the media of blacks as worthless, shiftless, lazy, incapable, criminal, infantile, and predisposed to violence and begin to believe them. More importantly, many of us recreate those images of ourselves through our words, thoughts, actions, and a perversion of "black" culture. Furthermore, with the advent of technology, we now mass-produce this internalized oppression for all to consume.

Perhaps one of the most significant social and cultural changes to take place during the post-civil rights era has been the attempt by blacks to reclaim black art and culture through the celebration of black music. Among the most successful and controversial has been the emergence of rap music.[132]

---

[132] Some critics will, no doubt, criticize my generic use of the term "rap music" as overbroad, in that I do not distinguish between "gansta rap," "hip-hop," and the wider hip-hop culture. They will also accuse me of having engaged in a superficial and cursory analysis of the genre that they claim is overly complex and fraught with contradictions. My response is

[50 Cent]
Nigga, Nigga i got hoes
I got hoes
[Chorus-50 Cent]
I got hoes
I'm the one to commit to a girl, from what a pimp
    come in drive to the world
I got hoes
There's so many places to see and things to do when
    ya fuckin with me
I got hoes
Every kind of bitch you like, come to the crib we
    gonn' party tonight
I got hoes
I got big ones, tall ones, small ones
I got thick ones, thin ones, call one
Tell her come on over i'll spoil her, and break bread
[Verse-50 Cent]
She can have blonde hair, blue eyes, vanilla thighs,
    I'm with it
Overseas, Japanese, rape to please, i get it
Yea up in the Israel the pussy is real
A bitch strap a bomb to the pussy and kill
I have freak bitches in Greece, Greek bitches in Niece
You can hear me from the next room 50 a piece
Call me Long John Silver, i breast stroke, back stroke
Pro swimmer, find out after dinner
Had a mixed bitch, half black, half Hawaiian

---

simple: This is not an attempt to deconstruct the so-called complexities. Many people have already done that. My intent instead is to demonstrate that rap music and its attendant videos and "lifestyle" collude with Jim Crow on steroids and bear some responsibility for its durability. I reject the notion that rap music should be given a "black pass" because it was written "by us, for us, or about us." Moreover, I also reject the trite and uncritical commentary that I am "blaming the victim." Rappers and their supporters are not without agency in their racist, sexist, and homophobic craft, which they peddle without apology or shame.

Half the time she told the truth the other half she was
    lyin
Yea i fucked models in London, they sold the story
I was gonna tell everybody they just told it for me
Please believe me, i'm a P-I-M-P
My dick shakin and makin a bitch look enzy
It's my G man, i mean my flow so hot
It make bitches in Bankok wanna bang cock
[Chorus-50 Cent]
I got hoes
I'm the one to commit to a girl, from what a pimp
    come in drive to the world
I got hoes
There's so many places to see and things to do when
    ya fuckin with me
I got hoes
Every kind of bitch you like, come to the crib we
    gonn' party tonight
I got hoes
I got big ones, tall ones, small ones
 I got thick ones, thin ones, call one
Tell her come on over i'll spoil her, and break bread
[Verse-Hot Rod]
The Jewels cost 500 grand
Turn the Murcielago engine of man, slide into the
    Lamb'
Whip the Ferrar so hard, Jake gave me ass a domestic
    charge
Nah nigga, i ain't no popeyed nigga
Drama or no baby momma nigga
Got a G on the necklace
Move sumthin out the jeans bitch better pet this or get
    the steppin
I got bills, bitch do somethin
Don't waste my time like quarterback mills
Just chill, wrist on ya forehead
Ride wit 4 niggas bitch give all four head

Yea hoe, you know i'm a pimp
7 tray duprees ride with a limp
Nuthin worse than a broke niggas whos a simp'
Fif call em monkeys, i call em chimps
Hold up man, i dropped my dollars
Bitch pick it up, and my pop my collar
[Chorus-50 Cent]
I got hoes
I'm the one to commit to a girl, from what a pimp
    come in drive to the world
I got hoes
There's so many places to see and things to do when
    ya fuckin with me
I got hoes
Every kind of bitch you like, come to the crib we
    gonn' party tonight
I got hoes
I got big ones, tall ones, small ones
I got thick ones, thin ones, call one
Tell her come on over i'll spoil her, and break bread
I got hoes
[50 Cent]
Niggas i got hoes, and that there is fa' sho fa' sho
I got hoes
Banks tell em i got hoes,
Yayo tell em i got hoes
I got hoes
Buck tell em i got hoes, Hot Rod tell em i got hoes
I got hoes
Nigga i got hoes, i ain't bullshittin i got hoes
I got hoes
Spider know i got hoes, M.O.P. know i got hoes
Mobb Deep know i got hoes, Eminem know i got hoes
Dr. Dre know i got hoes, Lord knows, i got hoes [133]

[133] 50 Cent Feat Hot Rod, "I Got Hoes," *DJ White Owl & 50 Cent-Fully Loaded-Mixfiend* (2007).

Who could have foreseen that as a result of the civil rights movement, some blacks would revel in the right to reinvigorate the hypersexual black male and claim this reclamation to be a sign of progress? Who would have thought that so many of us would claim that the civil rights movement gave us the right to call our black women bitches and hoes with pride and wanton abandon.

What I argue in this chapter is that for all the talk by rapademics,[134] social critics, and others about the socially, politically, and economically redeeming value of rap music, there has been no revolution. There has, however, been regression. Rappers, according to some rapademics, are supposedly reinvigorating the historical struggles of blacks in America and purveying it to a new generation of both blacks and whites. As tempting as this thesis is to accept, it simply does not comport with reality, largely because revolutions produce results. Where are the results that have been produced by rap's attempt to reclaim black history? Perhaps, the reclaiming is reclaiming old songs and giving them "Gangsta life." Consider the remake of the soul classical "Ain't no Woman."

> Foxy Brown: Ain't no nigga like the one I got
>
> Jay-Z: No one can fuck you better
>
> Foxy Brown: He sleeps around but he gives me a lot
>
> Jay Z: Keep you in diamonds and leather
>
> Jay Z: Ain't no stoppin' this, no lie. Promise to stay monogamous, I try. But love you know these hoes be makin' me weak. Y'all know how it goes so I stay deep.
>
> Foxy Brown: What up boo, just keep me laced in the illest snakes
>
> Bankrolls and shit
>
> Back rubs in the French tub
>
> Mackinest bitch, wifey Nigga
>
> So when you flip that coke
>
> 'member them days you was dead broke
>
> But now you stylin' I raised you

---

[134] I fundamentally believe that rap music should be the source of academic research and study. I also believe that such study should be done in a critical, thorough, and sifting way.

Basically made you into a don flippin' weight,
hero'n and shit.[135]

The current state of rap music and its carnage is less movement and more retrenchment. That is, it has produced temporal wealth for the black rappers, and sustainable wealth for the white executives, producers, and conglomerates that profit as we wallow shamelessly in self-denigration and debasement. Moreover, the MC's have willingly and indelibly etched in the world's minds the image of black women as a permanent and incorrigible class of nymphomaniac bitches and hoes, black men as disembodied penises, and "bling bling" as a proxy for success.[136] To be sure, not all rap or hip-hop music has done this. However, too much of hip-hop and rap music has. More importantly, there is now an entire generation of young black men for whom penis, womanizing, and masculinity are inextricably linked. Rap is the new crack.

Rap has taken some of the worst stereotypes of black men and women and lyrically and graphically injected them with steroids. The result is that Zips, Coons, Sambos, and thugs are seen as the very pinnacle of black male virility and achievement. To be successful in the wrap lexicon means to grab your dick (presumably to make it look bigger), to "fuck as many hoes as you can," to have been in jail, to brandish guns, to swim in bling and to be the baddest nigger in the streets. Black Entertainment Television has come to stand for Black Entertaining Thuggery. The black women who "shake that ass to show us what they workin' with," those who encourage the world to "lick their neck, their back, their pussy, and their crack," as well as those who parade virtually naked and unabashedly gyrate through the rap videos have colluded with the artists and other purveyors of black debasement. The videos could not be made without their willing participation. The black women in these videos have agency. They have exercised that agency

---

[135] Jay-Z, "Ain't No Nigga," *Reasonable Doubt* (1996).

[136] I will not engage in the argument about whether blacks created these images or not. Nor will I debate whether being black gives us the "right" to purvey these images, because I do not believe that this debate responds to the critical question of our agency in this regard. Moreover, regardless of whether we created these images or not, we have to ask ourselves what our responsibility is in purveying them to the next generation.

not to vindicate black womanhood, but to further defile it. The mammy has been replaced by the video hoe. The outcome of the rap movement has been to create a generation of pimps, hoes, and thugs defined by sexual deviance, female domination, and reified buffoonery. Lil' Kim sums it up:

> I used to pack Macs in Cadillacs
> Now I pimp gats in the ac's
> Watch my niggas backs
> Nine in the stores
> Glocks in the bags
> Maxing mini markets getting' money with the A-rabs
> No question confession
> Yes it's the lyrical
> Bitches squeeze your tits
> Niggas grab your genitals
> Proteins and minerals
> Exclude subliminals
> Big mama shots the game to all you fillies and crimi-
> nals...
> Bitches love the way I bust a rhyme
> 'Cause they all in line
> Screaming' "one more time!"
> Niggas
> Grab your dick if you love hip hop
> Bitches rub a dub in the back of the club, straight up.[137]

The problem with this is that Sojouner Truth fought for her black womanhood only to be disrespected, denigrated, and dehumanized not by whites but by black rappers. Perhaps they should consider So-jouner's fight:

> That many over there say that women needs to be helped into carriages, and lifted over ditches, and to have the best place everywhere. Nobody ever helps into carriages or over mud-puddles, or give me any best place! And ain't I a woman?

---

[137] Junior M.A.F.I.A., "Player's Anthem," *Conspiracy* (Big Beat 1995).

Look at me? Look at my arm? I have ploughed, and planted and gathered into barns, and no man could head me! And ain't I a woman? I could work as much as a man and eat as much as a man-when I could get it- and bear the lash as well! And ain't I a woman? I have borne thirteen children and seen 'em mos' all sold off to slavery, and when I cried out with my mother's grief, none but Jesus heard me! And ain't I a woman?[138]

Too many black men have readily accepted the notion that to be black, male, and masculine requires an absurd and hyperbolic carica- ture, which is steeped in thuggery, penis-centrism, and irresponsibility. Men who embrace this caricature define manhood by the size of one's penis (real or imagined); dress in a way that exposes the cracks of their asses, and do not take responsibility for the children they produce. The so-called "hip-hop generation" or "hip-hop culture" personifies and validates this caricature.

I am not an expert on rap, hip-hop, gansta rap, or all of their per- mutations, nor do I pretend to be. My point is simply that any discus- sion about the caricature being put forth to define black men is, in many cases, being written, produced, and starred in by black men, and must be unpacked if we are to understand the issue of black male mas- culinity. No doubt, many critics will castigate me for failing to under- stand the differences and sodalities of rap. To them I say, castigate away; and while you are doing so, unpack the images, have an honest conversation about them, and ask yourself how these images are differ- ent from Buck, Sambo, and the like.

Forman and Neal offer a spirited defense of hip-hop in *That's the Joint: the Hip Hop Studies Reader*. Writing about the problem of au- thenticity and the ethnographic imagination, they say: "When we try to apply the same principles to people with higher incomes, who are pre- sumed to be 'functional' and 'normative' we ultimately expose the ab- surdity of it all."[139] The problem, of course, is that as it relates specifi- cally to the topic of black male masculinity, hip-hop is neither func-

---

[138] Sojourner Truth, "Ain't I A Woman?" speech, Women's Conven- tion, Akron, Ohio, 1851.

[139] Murray Foreman and Mark Anthony Neal, eds., *That's the Joint! The Hip-Hop Studies Reader* (New York: Rutledge, 2004).

tional nor normative. It is instead constrained by its base, uncritical, exaggerated, internalized oppression, and the durable effects of slavery, Jim Crow, and the like. It is the Jim Crow moniker of hip-hop that is used to market it as progressive. Regardless of whether one agrees or disagrees with this conclusion, it is difficult to argue that any discussion about the black male caricature constructions can take place without a thorough and sifting analysis; too many of these images have become a perverted proxy for black success.

> Hip-hop has sustained a revolutionary current with respect to consumer culture despite the fact that it has become the most popular music in the United States. This revolutionary current exists in the underground communities of unsigned artists who push forward creative development without corporate involvement. They are cultural workers and artists in the organic sense, and proprietors of their own images. Local underground artists provide a good source when we seek feminists and other politically progressive messages in hip hop.[140]

For all of the talk by academics, social critics, and others about the socially and politically redeeming value of hip-hop, where is the revolution? Artists in this genre are supposedly reinvigorating the historical struggles of blacks in America and purveying such struggles to a new, unhistoricized generation. If so, what are the deliverables? Hypersexual masculinity? For all of its limitations, the civil rights movement was a revolution which led to changes in the social, political, economic and legal lives of blacks. Hip-hop has not led to any such revolution. Instead, much of the art that has been produced from this genre has taken some of the most vile and base stereotypes of black men and personified them. Black men are encouraged, through the visuals and vernacular of the hip-hop lifestyle, to prove their manhood by publicly displaying their underwear-covered asses in an unapologetic, homoerotic fashion for all the world to see. The Negro on the slave block has been replaced by the half-naked brother on the block. The reality is that we are using our power and freedom to create our own image to produce one of black male buffoonery and masculinity and making this the

---

[140] Imani Perry, *Prophets of the Hood: Politics and Poetics in Hip Hop* (Duke University Press, 2004) 188.

norm. Thus, whites can sit back and revel in our destruction with ostensibly clean hands.

Regardless of whether some believe that this is a result of the lingering effects of slavery or internalized oppression, I say, "Enough." Black men must understand the currency in race and gender subordination if we are to address our own racial demons.

> Race is a form of pleasure. For whites, it is a sadistic pleasure in decorating black bodies with disdain. For blacks—in today's non-revolutionary situation—it has become a masochistic pleasure in being so decorated. Oppressors require an Other in order to imagine themselves as elite. The system acquires its stability from the desires it cultivates in its perpetually excluded Others. The green light over the bay, like the Civil Rights Movement longing for equal rights and inclusion ('diversity') within this oppressive order of things, is a form of longing that links oppressed to oppressor at levels too deep for the mind to touch.[141]

Black male masculinity is contested space by both the oppressed and the oppressor and it requires a serious and reflective examination by black men for black men. This is a necessary prerequisite that will allow black men to begin the process of unpacking hegemonic masculinity and creating a masculinity that is not developed with an internalized oppression mindset and implemented as a result of slavery. It is difficult to understand gender when the hegemonic masculinity model places so little emphasis on the fact that men are also gendered.

Of course, there are many who will disagree with my choice not to present a simplistic, uncritical, pathological victimology defense of hip hop culture; Errol Henderson writes:

> Many African American youth are struggling around issues of manhood and womanhood. These definitions are rooted in identity. Identities are derived from culture. Definitions of manhood and womanhood (more specific identities) are derived from culture. If, as in the African American community, you have people who have been denied their culture by White supremacism, and youth who believe they have no culture, the

---

[141] Anthony Paul Farley, "The Black Body as Fresh Object," *Oregon Law Review* 76 (1997): 457.

African American community will devise one for themselves. Therefore, you will have a "hip-hop" culture full of youth with definitions of their identity and the rites of passage into manhood/womanhood defined by Euro-American guns, drug retailing, foreign made gym shoes, White distributed music, 40s, sexism, and misguided pronouncements of righteousness. Moreover, you will have the glamorization of the killing of other African Americans. Youth will know Tupac Shakur and glamorize or rationalize his self-destructive "thug life" but remain ignorant of Mutulu and Afeni Shakur. It is not hip-hop's responsibility to change all of this; that burden falls upon us all. It is the responsibility of all artists of oppressed groups to speak meaningfully in their art, sometime, someplace, to the liberation of their people.[142]

This statement simply misses the point. The point is that whites are not engaged in some secret plot to deny blacks black identity and culture. In modern day America hip hop has taken the opportunity to develop and purvey a culture based on guns, drugs, and penises. The artists, the producers and the video hoes are accountable for this creation, exportation, and rearticulation of this culture. We hold whites accountable for slavery and we need to hold hip hop accountable for the reinvigoration of the "nigger rap culture."

THE RAP ON REPARATIONS

There are many definitions of reparations and many different circumstances under which reparations can be granted or denied; and there are advocates and opponents of reparations. Definitions of reparations are both vague and recondite. However, the 1928 Permanent Court of International Justice provided guidelines that are useful in any reparations frame. In its ruling in the *Chorzów Factory* case, the court said that, "reparation must, so far as possible, wipe out all the consequences of the illegal act and reestablish the situation that would, in all probability, have existed if that act had not been committed." Compensation involves monetary payment for material or moral injury, while satisfaction addresses non-material injuries

---

[142] Errol A. Henderson, "Black Nationalism and Rap Music," *Journal of Black Studies* (Jan. 1996), 10 May 2008 <www.nbufront. org/html/fvwin98/erroll.html>.

and may involve official apologies, assurances of non-repetition of the offense, judicial proceedings, and truth and reconciliation commissions.[143] Although widely discussed in the context of slavery with an emphasis on the transatlantic slave trade and reparations for slavery for blacks in America, reparation has a history outside this discourse. France paid Germany 5 billion gold Francs as reparations after the Franco-Prussian War of 1872.[144] Germany paid France reparations after World War I, and the Soviet zone of Germany paid reparations to the Soviet Union after World War II.[145] Iraq is still paying reparations for the devastation that it caused during the Gulf War.[146]

The argument for reparations for slavery and its lingering effects has both its supporters and detractors. Central to the argument in favor of reparations is that the United States must make blacks whole for the losses they have endured as a result of slavery. Slavery and racism are responsible for the retardation of black culture and its continued internalized oppression. This argument correctly assumes that the institution of slavery has created an aura of dependence, as opposed to self-determination, which of course is detrimental to a collective and must be addressed. This is precisely what makes the argument so powerful.

> Compensation to Blacks for the injustices suffered by them must first and foremost be monetary. It must be sufficient to indicate that the United States truly wishes to make Blacks

---

[143] D. Shelton, "Righting Wrongs: Reparations in the Articles on State Responsibility," *American Journal of International Law* 96.4 (2002): 833–856.

[144] Michael Gavin, "Intertemporal Dimensions of International Economic Adjustment: Evidence from the Franco-Prussian War Indemnity," *The American Economic Review*, 82.2, Papers and Proceedings of the Hundred and Fourth Annual Meeting of the American Economic Association (May 1992): 174–179.

[145] Bruce Kuklick, *American Policy and the Division of Germany: The Clash with Russia over Reparations* (Ithaca, New York: Cornell University Press, 1972) 205.

[146] Rodney J. Morrison, "Gulf War Reparations: Iraq, OPEC, and the Transfer Problem," *American Journal of Economics and Sociology*, 51.4 (Oct. 1992): 385–399.

whole for the losses they have endured. Sufficient, in other words, to reflect not only the extent of unjust Black suffering, but also the need for Black economic independence from societal discrimination. No less than with the freedmen, freedom for Black people today means economic freedom and security. A basis for that freedom and security can be assured through group reparations in the form of monetary compensation, along with free provision of goods and services to Black communities across the nation. The guiding principle of reparations must be self-determination in every sphere of life in which Blacks are currently dependent.

To this end, a private trust should be established for the benefit of all Black Americans. The trust should be administered by trustees popularly elected by the intended beneficiaries of the trust. The trust should be financed by funds drawn annually from the general revenue of the United States for a period not to exceed ten years. The trust funds should be expendable on any project or pursuit aimed at the educational and economic empowerment of the trust beneficiaries to be determined on the basis of need. Any trust beneficiary should have the right to submit proposals to the trustees for the expenditure of trust funds.

The above is only a suggestion about how to use group reparations for the benefit of Blacks as a whole. In the end, determining a method by which all Black people can participate in their own empowerment will require a much more refined instrument than it would be appropriate for me to attempt to describe here. My own beliefs about what institutions Black people need most certainly will not reflect the views of all Black people, just as my belief that individual compensation is not the best way to proceed probably does not place me in the majority. Everybody who could just get a check has many reasons to believe that it would be best to get a check. On this point, I must subscribe to the wisdom that holds, if you give a man a loaf, you feed him for a day. It is for those Blacks who survive on a "breadconcern level" that the demand for reparations assumes its greatest importance.[147]

In some respects, the effects of slavery and rap music can and should be compared as part of the discussion of reparations. Slavery kept blacks in bondage, both physically and mentally; some forms of rap music do the same. Slavery relied on the purveyance of vile and subhuman caricatures of blacks to keep slavery alive; some rap music does the same. Slavery disrespected black women and black men; some rap music does the same. Slavery was an economic system in which the master profited and the slaves worked the fields; rap music does the same. Slavery was an institution of economic disenfranchisement; rap music is also.

So, where is the hue and cry for reparations for rap music? Where is the compensation fund that will be set up to pay for the lost generations of black boys and black girls? Why have civil rights organizations such as the NAACP and others not called for reparations for rap music? Maybe it is because they want the corporations that make money from rap music, much as the plantation owners made money from the blacks who worked the field, to fund their irrelevance. Along with the scourge of racism, economic disenfranchisement, internalized oppression, poverty, and America's failure to act decisively to end discrimination in an honest and deliberate way, the lack of a serious discussion of reparations for rap music, which denigrates black women and men, is the human rights issue of our time.

---

[147] Robert Westley, "Many Billions Gone: Is It Time to Reconsider the Case for Black Reparations?" *Boston College Law Review* XL.1 (Dec. 1998): 429.

CHAPTER TEN
RACE IS A STATE OF MIND

Having introduced the abandonment of human rights by the NAACP and a framework for understanding and discussing hegemonic masculinity, I turn now to a discussion of racial thinking. This is not an exhaustive review of race and the articulation of difference; nor is it a complete history of the normative character of race. It is instead intended to provide readers with language with which to talk about race. It is also intended to make the point that the contours of race in America have been constructed, limited, and rearticulated through both a sociological and legal lens. Moreover, since the NAACP accepted the position that equality could only be vindicated through the American legal system, race in America cannot be understood or analyzed without a significant understanding of the interplay of race and the legal system.

> We hold these truths to be self-evident: That all men are created equal; that they are endowed by their Creator with certain unalienable rights; that among these are life, liberty, and the pursuit of happiness [. . .][148]

Despite these affirmative claims of equality in the Declaration of Independence, America saw no inherent contradiction in declaring independence on the one hand, and procuring and enslaving blacks on the other. Nor did the founding fathers see any contradictions in constructing and then making normative the binary categories of white and

---

[148] Thomas Jefferson, Declaration of Independence of the United States of America, preamble, 1776.

black. The founding fathers also did not hold it to be self-evident that there was an organic injustice in the subordination of blacks and attendant declaration of the supremacy of whites. "Categories such as Indians and Negroes were invented in the sixteenth and seventeenth centuries to justify the continued exploitation of people."[149]

> The invention of such categories entails a dialectical process of construction; that is, the creation of the category 'Other' involves the creation of the category same. If 'Indians' are depicted as 'savages,' Europeans are characterized as 'civilized;' 'blacks' are defined as natural candidates for slavery, 'whites' are defined as free subjects.[150]

In fact, the normative and binary constructions were subsequently used to justify the declaration of blacks as not equal, and thus not to be endowed with inalienable rights. These constructions were not only made by individuals, they were supported by institutions, such as the courts which sanctioned and in fact reified the inequality of blacks. In the famous *Dred Scott* case, the United States Supreme Court said:

> The words 'people of The United States' and 'citizens' are synonymous terms, and mean the same thing. They both describe the political body, who according to our republican institutions, form the sovereignty, and who hold the power and conduct Government through their representatives. They are what we familiarly call the 'sovereign people,' and every citizen is one of these people, and a constituent, member of this sovereignty. The question before us is whether the classes of persons described in the plea in abatement compose a portion of this people, and are constituent members of this sovereignty? We think that they are not, and that they are not in-

---

[149] On the invention of the white race, see Theodore W. Allen, *The Invention of the White Race*, I (London: Verso, 1994). On the invention of the Indian race, see, Robert E. Berkhoffer, *The White Man's Indian* (New York: Vintage, 1978). On the invention of the black and white races, see Winthrop D. Jordan, *White Over Black: American Attitudes Toward the Negro, 1550–1812* (Chapel Hill, North Carolina: University of North Carolina Press, 1995).

[150] Thomas Gossett, *Race: The History of An Idea in America* (Dallas: Southern Methodist University Press, 1963).

cluded, and were not intended to be included, in the word 'citizens' in the Constitution, and can therefore claim none of the rights and privileges which that instrument provides for and secures for citizens of The United States. On the contrary, they were at that time subordinate and inferior class of beings, who had been subjugated by the dominant race.[151]

Given express authority to do so by the state, individual actors and social institutions freely colluded to codify individual prejudices and biases to create and fortify racialized social systems. This codification and organization of social systems around socially constructed and accepted notions of race was instrumental in racializing American society. After a society becomes racialized, racialization develops a life of its own.[152] Modern-day white America has benefited and continues to benefit from racialization and its lingering effects, while modern-day black America continues to suffer. In a formalistic and legalistic sense, America has removed racialized distinctions to the extent that they, at least on their face, seek to perpetuate racism. The removal of formalistic and legalistic barriers has not, however, had the effect of completely fulfilling the promise of equality as enunciated in the Declaration of Independence and the United States Constitution. America continues to struggle to fulfill these promises of equality.

Neoconservatives, class theorists, and the neo-left disagree as to whether the promises remain unfulfilled. While it is clear that these groups have political and ideological differences on the subject of race, they also have doctrinal differences as well. That is, neoconservative scholars, class theorists, and neo-left thinkers disagree on the meaning and continued significance of race and racism in present-day America. These disagreements are not mere abstractions. They are instead, disagreements about how, if at all, black lives and progress continue to be affected by the effects of slavery.

I will examine and critique the neoconservative position, as well as the positions of the class theorists and neo-left. I will also argue for a deconstruction of racism that is anti-subordinationist in nature, in that it

---

[151] Dred Scott v. Sandford.

[152] Eugene Genovese, *Red and Black: Marxian Explorations in Southern and Afroamerican History* (New York: Pantheon, 1980).

seeks to produce a more complete explanation of the continued significance of race and the continuing effects of racism in America.

BOOTSTRAPPING, VICTIMOLOGY, AND COLORBLINDNESS: THE NEOCONSERVATIVE VIEW

Neoconservatives take the view that racism is less relevant today in determining the quality of lives for blacks and their potential success than ever before. For many neoconservatives, racism in modern-day America has gone the way of Jim Crow and separate but equal. In their view, blacks can live where they want, work where they want, go to school where they want, marry whom they want, and be anything they want to be. Many neoconservatives do not see black people; they simply see people. They believe that blacks should not be African-Americans; they should simply be Americans. To support this view, many neoconservative commentators and scholars quote Martin Luther King who argued for judging people not by the color of their skin, but by the content of their character. Neoconservatives believe Martin Luther King argued not for a color conscious society, but for a color-blind society. Thus, neoconservatives can claim that their doctrinal view of civil rights is steeped in Dr. King's philosophy and rhetoric.

Neoconservatives are not only white. In fact, there are neoconservative black scholars who subscribe to and promulgate a bootstrapping ideology. The bootstrapping ideology, simply stated, is that since racism and segregation have been outlawed, blacks must pull themselves up by their own proverbial bootstraps. As evidence of the declining significance of race in the lives of blacks, neoconservative scholars often point to the many demographic and economic studies comparing the status of blacks and whites in terms of income, occupation, health, and education. They argue these show an almost epic reduction in racial inequality in the United States as a result of the removal of formal racial barriers.[153, 154]

---

[153] Otis A. Duncan, "Patterns of Occupational Mobility Among Negro Men," *Demography* 5.1 (1968): 11–22.

[154] James P. Smith and Finnis R. Welch, *Closing the Gap: Forty Years of Economic Progress for Blacks* (Santa Monica: Rand, 1986).

The neoconservative scholar who is the darling of the movement is Thomas Sowell. In Sowell's view, racial prejudice cannot explain the low income of the American black population. Sowell situates racism in the past.

> Blanket application of the term 'racism' as a *causal* explanation—as distinguished from simply an epithet—cannot explain why blacks who were living in white neighborhoods at the beginning of the twentieth century could no longer do so two decades later or five decades later. After all, those who interspersed among whites in the earlier period were of the same race as those who could not do so in the middle of the twentieth century.[155]

In addition, Sowell believes that the struggle for civil rights is in fact largely to blame for the current plight of blacks in the United States. More specifically, he laments what he calls "the civil rights vision." According to Sowell, this view developed as the leaders of the civil rights movement shifted the movement's original focus on equal treatment under the law to a demand for equal rights notwithstanding genuine differences in ability, thereby legitimatizing the movement's claim in a democratic society. In Sowell's view, the civil rights vision is regressive in nature and largely inapplicable to issues of racism today because "the battle for civil rights was fought and won—at great cost—many years ago."[156] Moreover, Sowell sees the central problem of modern-day American blacks not to be racism, but white liberals. In Sowell's view,

> [b]y projecting a vision of a world in which the problems of blacks are consequences of the actions of whites, either immediately or in times past, white liberals have provided a blanket excuse for shortcomings and even crimes by blacks. The very possibility of any *internal* cultural sources of the problems of

---

[155] Thomas Sowell, *Black Rednecks, White Liberals* (San Francisco: Encounter Books, 2005) 61.

[156] Thomas Sowell, *Civil Rights: Rhetoric or Reality?* (New York: Harper Collins, 1984) 109.

blacks have been banished from consideration by the fashion-
able phrase *blaming the victim.*[157]

Sowell goes on to say:

> [e]xternal explanations of black-white differences—
> discrimination or poverty for example—seem to many to be
> more amenable to public policy than internal explanations such
> as culture. Those with this point of view tend to resist cultural
> explanations but there is yet another reason why some resist
> understanding the counterproductive effect of an anachronistic
> culture: Alternative explanations of economic and social lags
> on the sins of others, such as racism or discrimination. Equally
> important, such external explanations require no internal
> changes in the black population but leave all changes to
> whites, who are seen as needing to be harangued, threatened,
> or otherwise forced to change.[158]

Sowell's central argument is that the battle against racism has already been fought and won. In the present day, the culprit is not racism,
it is instead liberal whites who have constructed a politically correct
discourse, as well as blacks who are culturally inferior and refuse to
help themselves. These individuals collude with liberal whites to blame
all of their shortcomings on their victim status, instead of their culturally insidious ways.

In addition, Sowell believes that there are central differences between whites and blacks and that these differences are not a product of
racism, they are a fact of life. Sowell argues the foundation for black
institutional victimology and white liberal complicity has been built on
what he perceives to be an illegitimate civil rights claim for equality of
results, without consideration for the genuine, innate differences in
abilities between whites and blacks.

The neoconservative position is clear. Racism was something that
occurred in the past and so blacks cannot blame their continued disenfranchisement on racism. Moreover, white liberals are complicit in creating and sustaining a pathological victimology and blacks have latched
on to this. Mona Charen, Sowell's colleague agrees:

---

[157] Sowell, *Black Rednecks, White Liberals,* 52.

[158] Sowell, *Black Rednecks, White Liberals,* 62.

Not only does this insult honorable white people who have banished racism from polite society, it does incalculable damage to the morale of black Americans. The stoking of racial animus is evidence of the way liberals harm those they claim to want to help. It further undermines black progress by diverting attention away from the true problems of the twenty-first-century America—problems such as disintegrating families, weak schools, and the multicultarist assault on American-identity—while do-gooder Don Quioxtes ostentatiously swing as white racist windmills.[159]

In the neoconservative view, the promise of equality has largely been fulfilled. It is not equality that is the problem; it is the failure of blacks to take advantage of that equality that is the problem. Racism is situated in the past and so then is discrimination. The neoconservatives view America as a society happily on its way to the promised equality. They offer as evidence of equality social and economic transformation, policies addressing discrimination, and a significant reduction in raw, invidious discrimination and racism. They laud what they term more inclusive and egalitarian social arrangements.

CEMENT BOOT STRAPS AND DECONTEXTUALIZATION: A CRITIQUE OF THE NEOCONSERVATIVE VIEW

The central problem with the neoconservative position is that it assumes that the elimination of formalistic racism means that blacks who did not have boots—much less bootstraps—during formal segregation have now been given them, and thus, should be prepared to pull themselves up. It also assumes that the elimination of a formal system of subordination means that the lingering effects of racism have simply disappeared. This is clearly an untenable position for three primary reasons.

First, racism is not a single issue, so equal treatment according to "neutral" norms is by definition limited to the whims of individual actors in individual situations. Second, at the institutional level, the legalistic elimination of racial segregation has not resulted in the concomi-

---

[159] Mona Charen, *Do-Gooders: How Liberals Hurt Those They Claim to Help (and the Rest of Us)*, (New York, New York: Penguin Group, Dec. 2004) 69.

tant promulgation and enforcement of social policy, which if the logic holds up (and it has not) would result in the equal treatment of blacks. Finally, modern-day racism in the neoconservative paradigm is analyzed and discussed without reference to history and context, resulting in an analysis that is limited in both scope and application.

To accept the neoconservative view, one would have to believe that the only legitimate and effective means of ensuring a racially equitable society is the destruction of formal systems of subordination and discrimination. The analytical difficulty with adopting this belief is that even though these formalistic barriers have been dismantled, the people who administer the new systems continue to assign largely positive meaning to white and largely negative meaning to black. So, the neoconservative preference for a move to a color-blind society and equal process is simply a romanticized notion of the promise of equality. This romance with color-blindness is simply out of place in a society in which blacks have actually been treated differently on the basis of race and this difference in treatment continues into the present, largely devoid of racial pejoratives, but with markers that, while not outwardly racially vitriolic, are vitriolic in effect.

The neoconservatives have simply placed a higher value on form over substance. This paradigm is neither a critical look at race and racism nor a rationale for why we should accept an aracial contextualization of race. So, their position is of limited value in understanding the current status of the march toward equality. Moreover, people such as Charen insist on giving whites credit for being noble in their alleged banishment of racism from society. There are significant problems with this.

First, it strikes me as odd that working to eliminate racism would be noble at all. The very use of the word noble suggests that Charen believes that eliminating racism is not right because it is morally right, but that it is right because whites who purveyed it and enshrined it into law decided, for political and economic reasons, to get rid of it. This is arrogance not nobility.

Second, neoconservatives stoke racial animus to win elections in America all the time. Consider that neoconservative groups wanted to change the public perception of former President George H. W. Bush in his campaign against Michael Dukakis. Politically, Bush had the problem of running in the shadows of the very popular President Reagan. The fact was that no sitting vice-president since Martin Van Buren in 1836 had been elected to the presidential slot outright. Opinion polls at the time showed a very favorable public perception of Dukakis.

Faced with history and the positive opinions of his opponent, "independent" political groups (527s) decided to play the race card. They developed an ad that revived the image of Gus, the menacing black man in *Birth of A Nation*. Willie Horton was a convicted killer who had escaped while on furlough from a Massachusett's prison and killed a white couple. The photograph of Willie Horton was minacious with his afro and darkened features—every white person's worst fear. The ostensibly neutral reason for airing the ad was to portray Dukakis as soft on crime. Fair enough. The problem, however, was that if the ad was to be believed, Dukakis also granted furloughs to white prisoners. So why was the "menacing" black man the subject of the ad? The answer is that many neoconservatives stoke racial animus to win presidential elections in America where the irrational fear of black men is still a reality. The ad worked and Bush won.

In addition to this Bush ad, more recently there was the ad that openly and notoriously raised the issue of miscegenation against Harold Ford, Jr. in his quest to be the first African-American to win the United States Senate seat from Tennessee. The ad, sponsored by the Republican National Committee, featured a scantily clad blonde actress who claims that she met Ford at a Playboy party. The ad ends with an overly seductive wink and her imploring, "Harold, call me." The message in 2006, in Tennessee was clear: White men cannot and should not put a black man in the Senate who has defiled a white woman. We cannot allow a black man to assume such a high political office, when he, like Silas Lynch in *Birth of a Nation,* only wants our pride and joy, the white woman. Up until the ad was run, Ford was either leading or tied with his white male opponent. Ford subsequently lost the race becoming the only Democrat in that election cycle to lose. This proves that stoking racial animus is, in fact, their electoral moniker. Does it do incalculable damage to the morale of white Americans when they do so? Or does white privilege allow them to opt out of this too?

Third, neoconservatives as a group dismiss the idea of institutionalized racism by confidently situating racism in the past. This allows them to have "black friends" and feel noble about their efforts. However, we live in a racialized society; therefore, it is simply intellectually bankrupt to suggest, and expect us to believe, that racism is in the past just because neoconservatives say so.

Having examined the neoconservative view, I now turn my focus toward a growing group of critics whom I term class theorists. Critics in this group view the status of black Americans in the context of class. I think it is important to examine this view, because discourse about equality and race in America is often limited by its over-reliance on the viewpoints of the left and right.

THE CLASS THEORISTS:
IT'S THE CLASS LINE, NOT THE COLOR LINE

Class theorists explain continuing racial inequality through a discourse that acknowledges, but then diminishes the relevance of race and racism to modern-day black life. They claim that the reason blacks have not attained promised equality is not race, but class. They believe that since some blacks have attained economic success, and thus access to opportunity, race loses its primacy and significance in determining the plight of blacks. That being the case, they posit, racism cannot explain why many blacks still remain at the bottom of the economic ladder. Class theorists argue that viewing race as central to determining the lives of blacks in modern America limits our comprehension of the central role that economic stratification plays in impacting modern black life. From their point of view, race and racism still exists in America; however, to understand why blacks have not attained promised equality, one cannot be stuck in the social reality and construct of the twentieth century. One must instead look at the plight of blacks through the lens of class and not race. For class theorists, racial inequality in post-civil rights, post-industrial revolution America has a degree of specificity and relevance that is marked by a class line and not a color line. The class theorists' position is best articulated by Professor William Julius Wilson:

> As the nation has entered the latter half of the twentieth century however, many of the traditional barriers have crumbled under the weight of the political, social, and economic changes of the civil rights era. A new set of obstacles has emerged from

basic structural shifts in the economy. These obstacles are therefore impersonal but may prove to be even more formidable for certain segments of the black population. Specifically, whereas the previous barriers were usually designed to control and restrict the entire black population, the new barriers create hardships essentially for the black underclass; whereas the old barriers were based explicitly on racial motivations derived from intergroup contact the new barriers have racial significance only in their consequences, not in their origins. In short, whereas the old barriers bore the pervasive features of racial oppression, the new barriers indicate an important and emerging form of class subordination.[160]

Thus, class theorists believe the centrality of race and racism is of limited value in understanding and explaining the problems of the black underclass. They posit that there is a need for a new paradigm for understanding the black underclass, because the "new barriers," are not explicitly racists, they are casually racists. "In the economic sphere, class had become more important than race in determining black access to privilege and power."[161] Wilson goes on to say that "it is equally clear that the black underclass is in a hopeless state of economic stagnation, falling further and further behind the rest of society."[162]

CRITIQUE OF THE CLASS THEORY

While there is no question that class is a consideration in modern-day America, it alone does not explain the continued disenfranchisement of blacks. To suggest, as the class theorists do that class has simply overtaken race as the issue, is to engage in a Hobbesian analysis of race and racism that simply cannot withstand scrutiny. Moreover, the reality is that white capitalists and white workers have different class

---

[160] William Julius Wilson, *The Declining Significance of Race: Blacks and Changing American Institutions* (Chicago: University of Chicago Press, 1980) 2.

[161] Wilson 2.

[162] Wilson 2.

interests, but they also have similar racial interests, since they both benefit from white supremacy.

Wilson's analysis fails largely because he discusses race and racism much like the neoconservatives. That is, to both groups racism is situated in the past and the outcomes of institutional racism are not acknowledged and analyzed with sufficient rigor. They are instead explained away. These two visions are premised upon a limited view of what racism is given a particular worldview. Thus, though they both attempt to lay claim to a new vantage point from which to analyze race and racism, they both rely on a limited view of how racism currently operates. The rhetoric establishing the removal of formal discrimination, as doubtful as it may be, is the foundation upon which both the neoconservatives and the class theorists have constructed their arguments.

There is no question that the passage of civil rights laws nurtured the impression that America has moved swiftly to end the oppression of blacks. The problem however, is the passage of laws alone cannot and did not achieve the reality of equality. Therefore, to suggest, as the class theorists do, that the new struggle is about class and not about race is to miss the point. The laws operated to end formal discrimination of the most invidious kind.

> By the nineteenth century, conventional casuallassumed the uncontroversial validity of a hierarchy of 'higher' and 'lower' of 'master' and 'subject' races for whom it is obvious, different rules must apply...[163]

The test, it seems, is to maintain a contextualized view of race and racism that is not constrained by rhetoric and hyperbole, but that understands and acknowledges the diversity of the ways in which blacks continue to experience racism and whites continue to benefit from it. It is not to simply replace one worldview with another.

> The formation of the racial groups in our midst must be understood on a social basis. In a community comprising two distinct types which are socially clearly separated, the social grouping is reinforced by the outer appearance of the individu-

---

[163] Charles W. Mills, *The Racial Contract* (Ithaca and London: Cornell University Press, 1997) 27.

als and each is at once and automatically assigned to his own group.[164]

VIEW FROM THE NEO-LEFT

Having presented and critiqued the class theorists' view, I turn now to what I term the neo-leftist view. Various scholars connected with this view present race and racism as problematic. The story of race and racism is told as if it has followed a natural progression. The neo-left weaves a tale that leads us to believe that we have come from a backwards time of measuring heads and assigning meaning to race to the current period in which integration is the ultimate goal. The neo-left position has given us programs such as affirmative action and has encouraged us to celebrate our diversity.

The neo-left philosophy was borne out of the civil rights movements when hundreds of thousands of people mobilized to challenge the political, economic, and cultural power relations in cities and towns across the country, employing tactics that included mass protests, economic boycotts, sit-ins, and strikes.[165] The neo-left believes that racism is fundamentally wrong and in some cases immoral. In this context, racism has come to be understood as a compromised set of attitudes and beliefs that support racist domination and the goals of racist justice. The concepts of prejudice, discrimination, and segregation are the key elements of this ideology. Each idea embodies a different manifestation of what is seen as the central aspect of racism—the distortion of reason through the prism of myth and ignorance.

From this perspective then, racism is firmly grounded in consciousness, in the cognitive process that attributes social significance to skin color. The key element here is one of irrationalism; the problem with prejudice is that it obscures the work of reason by clouding per-

---

[164] Franz Boas, *Anthropology and Modern Life* (New York: W.W. Norton, 1962) 71.

[165] Thomas R. Brooks, *Walls Come Tumbling Down: A History of the Civil Rights Movement: 1940–1970* (Englewood Cliffs, NJ: Prentice-Hall 1974).

ception with beliefs rooted in superstition.[166] The neo-left position sees integration as the solution. This view is best articulated by T. Cross:

> Integration is indispensable to shattering racial stereotypes. Only in day-to-day contacts with blacks will whites learn that blacks are not less intelligent, less honest or less human than whites. Through time, integrated living and integrated education are the most forceful weapons for breaking down the stubborn and enduring mental habit of defining people's traits according to their race.[167]

At the individual level, the neo-left considers equal treatment according to neutral norms the antidote for racism. At the institutional level, they view integration as the solution that will bring about change in the social system. In sum, individuals must stop discriminating and institutions should integrate. Once neutrality replaces discrimination, equal opportunity will lead to integrated institutions; experience in integrated institutions, will in turn, replace the ignorance of racism with the knowledge that actual contact provides. The integrationists' analysis of white supremacy ideology focuses on the failure of white supremacists to recognize that we are all the same; we simply come in different packages. According to this view, white racists perceive the world through a false structure of "same" and "different," which utilizes an analytic of blacks as different and denies that the attributes possessed by whites exist in blacks. Thus, the rationality and piousness that supposedly characterize whites are in racist ideology denied to blacks. The neo-left comprehends racism at a high level of abstraction, in part because they wish to transcend the bias of particularity, which they see as the root of race consciousness. It is the classic liberal philosophy, which connects truth, universalism, and progress.

CRITIQUE OF THE NEO-LEFT VIEW

Like the neoconservative view and the class theorists' view, there are serious limits to the neo-left view. The neo-left view is helpful in

---

[166] Robert Blauner, *Racial Oppression in America* (New York: Harper and Row, 1972) 19.

[167] Theodore L. Cross, *The Black Power Imperative: Racial Inequality and the Politics of Nonviolence* (New York: Faulkner, 1987) 609–610.

understanding the limits of integration. However, this view does not analyze racism as an ideological foundation upon which America is built and from which America continues to operate. The game is the same; the name is different. The neo-left position is problematic because it fails to account for the hegemonic role of racism in modern America. All three groups have fallen victim to identity politics, and thus, have failed to provide a useful framework from which to understand the problem of racism in America. "The problem with identity politics is not that it fails to transcend difference as some critics charge, but rather—the opposite—that it frequently conflates or ignores intragroup differences."[168]

There is no arguing, the formal removal of barriers to discrimination are a sign of progress and to suggest otherwise would simply not make sense. The problem, however, is that the neo-left, like the class theorists and the neoconservatives, treat the formal removal of barriers with much more reverence than it deserves. The removal of barriers, while significant, has not been sufficient to fulfill the promise of equality as described in the Declaration of Independence and the U.S. Constitution. We are instead left with a vacuous abstraction of racism and its impact on the lives of blacks. The neo-left has given us Affirmative Action programs that, though helpful for providing access, are steeped in the subordinationist language that they are supposed to be eviscerating. Among the arguments advanced for Affirmative Action is the following:

> Society may simply need to know that there are talented blacks and women, so that it does not automatically assign them lesser respect or status. We need to have unjustified stereotype beliefs replaced with more accurate ones about the talents of blacks and women. So we need to engage in preferential hiring of qualified minorities even when they are not the most qualified.[169]

---

[168] Kimberle Crenshaw, "Mapping the Margins: Intersectionality, Identity Politics, and Violence against Women of Color," *Stanford Law Review* 43.6 (Jul. 1991) 1241.

[169] Francis J. Beck, *Affirmative Action: Social Justice or Reverse Discrimination?* (Amherst, NY: Prometheus Books, 1997) 179.

Just listen to the neo-left commentators who are vehement in their discussions that Affirmative Action is about hiring "qualified minorities." This language assumes that racial minorities are in general unqualified and so to find a qualified black is the exception rather than the rule. Racial hierarchy cannot be removed simply by a move to "neutrality" and integration. The white norm has not disappeared; it has only been submerged in popular consciousness. The neo-left has simply repackaged it through the use of liberal views steeped in identity politics.

SELF-DEFINING IDENTITY POLITICS AND THE PROMISE OF EQUALITY

The challenge for blacks is to avoid boxing ourselves into a predefined set of identity politics that seek to tell us how racism affects us in a de-contextualized, ahistoricized manner. Instead, we must rethink the ways in which racism has been understood and codified in dominant discourse for the past several decades.

> Just as emerging structures of the new racism constitute a reformulation of former racial formations, the closing door of racial opportunity of the post-civil rights era also invokes ideas and practices about class, gender, and sexuality associated with the prior periods. All three past-in-present racial formations have effects that endure in the present and in the present are likely to persist, regardless of changes in ideology.[170]

We should therefore understand that formal equality is an abstraction in that we are told that we are equal under the law, yet in many of our lives that equality is illusive. We are told that we can compete for jobs in any sector and any industry, yet we face glass ceilings in many of these organizations. If formal equality is such a success, why then, in modern-day America, are we still celebrating the first black to do this or that? The reality is that, claims to the contrary notwithstanding, distribution of power and resources which were racially determined before the advent of formal equality continue to be distributed thus. Race is rearticulated in a manner that perpetuates the distribution of rights, privileges, and opportunity established under a regime of ongoing white

---

[170] Patricia Hill Collins, *Black Sexual Politics* (New York: Routledge, 2005) 84.

white supremacy that neither neoconservatives, class theorists, nor neo-leftists have attempted to deconstruct. Instead, each group has fashioned an ideology for explaining racism that simply reinforces their identity politics.

The challenge for blacks then is to create and embrace our own identity politics that is not clouded by the presence of formal equality, nor practiced out of blind loyalty to the neo-leftists. This position will encourage us to understand that even though race is a socially constructed category, its effects still have meaning. We must understand issues of racial ideology matter in America, despite promises of equality. This is not an easy task, and we must be mindful to avoid falling into the trap of racial thinking.

For blacks, the task at hand is to resist the temptation to become identified with racial thinking as constructed by each of the groups mentioned in this edition. To be sure, these groups contain both black and white scholars, and while each group purports to have eliminated racism, they have, in fact, made little more than a token effort to understand the reality of subordination and white supremacy in modern-day America.

Modern-day white supremacy is maintained not through racial invective and subordinative violence; it is instead maintained through the symbiotic and codependent relationship of colorblindness, class primacy, and integrationist ideology. These interdependent contributors have advanced a false sense of neutrality that many of us have latched onto without realizing that the new white supremacy is more dangerous than the old, in that its covert nature makes it much more difficult to attack. The fact is that race and the articulation of difference is significant not for what it says about race, but for what it does about race. That is, the new racism is just like the old racism, not in form, but in application. We cannot and will not attain real equality until we are comfortable being race-conscious rather than race-blind. Whites are, and thus, have achieved more than formal equality.

The issue of race is central to the United States and organizations such as the NAACP have been responsible for addressing race and making deals that ultimately formed and cemented racial thinking that is difficult to discard.

The new racialism differs from the scientific racialism that Du Bois was writing against, but both operate to explain racial differences with regards to material conditions, justifying them as the natural order of things; both turn a blind eye to the way these racial disparities were consciously (intentionally) and unconsciously (negligently, recklessly) constructed by individuals and institutions.[171]

America uses all types of media to form, cement, explain, purvey, and export racial differences. One of the most prominently used is film. Writing of Jayne Mansfield in the film *Felicity,* Anthony Paul Farley says, "in the film of the same name, we see Mansfield, improbably blond, busty, and slim-waisted, walk down the street in full color. We also see the men seeing her. A prepubescent paper boy whistles at her like an adult wolf; an iceman's supply simply melts under his hands and pours from the bed of his truck onto the street; milk spurts forth from a milk man's bottle and runs all over his hand; finally, the spectacles of a too-curious neighbor shatter as he gazes on her body."[172] Farley makes the point here that film uses its power to define race, to privilege whiteness over blackness and to cement those images into the minds and lives of Americans. Film then, is but another medium by which race and its meaning are articulated and rearticulated.

In the following section I discuss the interplay between law, race, and film to provide the reader with a greater understanding of the impact of film in keeping the issue of race alive.

---

[171] Francisco Valdes, Jerome McCristal Culp, and Angela P. Harris, eds., *Crossroads, Directions, and a New Critical Race Theory* (Philadelphia: Temple University Press, 2002) 12.

[172] Farley 457.

CHAPTER ELEVEN
ADDING SOME CONTEXT

Having provided a framework for discussing masculinity, I turn now to the medium of film, in which masculinity is constructed and articulated. Film, in the American context, is part of a collection of critical cultural and social mores. Film serves as both entertainment and social commentary, and can be used as propaganda. Filmmakers not only respond to masculinity and femininity, they often construct masculinity and femininity, and their films serve to reinforce firmly held beliefs and stereotypes and create new realities. It is often those realities that validate, and in some cases undermine, the societal and ideological place occupied or vacated by black men in America.

Ed Guerrero, in his work, "The Black Man on Our Screens and the Empty Space in Representation" writes that "sadly, and dangerously, for all of us as a diverse, multicultural society, we have constructed in our films and in our media in general, between the love-hate polarities of Bill Cosby and Willie Horton, a vast, empty space in representation." [173] Drawing on Guerrero's work of empty space, I want to expand the empty space metaphor. The empty space or representational void is not only a filmic portrayal, it has come to represent the way that some black men live their lives and how some social constructions reinforce that empty space.

This empty space had, and has, at least two facets. First, filmmakers who create the empty space and by their conscious decision to posit

---

[173] Ed Guerrero, "The Black Man on Our Screens and the Empty Space in Representation," *Callaloo* 18.2 (Spring 1995): 399.

the empty space, send the message that they have determined that black men must be either good or evil. What it means to be good or evil has both masculine and feminine implications. Given the strong and pervasive influence of film in shaping public opinions of all people and given that many people will never interact with a black man except on film, this allows filmmakers to control the image of black male masculinity well beyond the making of a movie.

The second facet is that the empty space ignores the diversity that exists among and between black men, as is true among and between all men. Guerrero's metaphor of the empty space raises, but does not answer, the question of whether there is enough cultural distinctiveness, and enough subordination by the empty space, that we must treat incomplete representations of black masculinity by filmmakers of all kinds as yet another tool in the quiver of racial subordination and oppression.

America is a visual society, and as such, many people intentionally or unintentionally rely on filmic images to shape their cultural and historical beliefs. When we consume these images, they also become real to us. We may be passive moviegoers, however, we are also active racial decision makers. Thus, ideology is formed and refined through a variety of media and mediums, including film.

Masculinity is a contested concept, as is what it means to be both black and masculine. Black masculinity is not only defined in relation to a dominant society by films, it is oppressed through that relational aspect. This is not merely an intellectual discussion. Ideology, whether created by film, reinforced by film, or formed as a result of our interactions with film, forms the basis of many of our decisions. A major challenge to American society is to unpack the components of ideology. That is, who gets to construct "American ideology"? What roles do the realities of race, class, and subordination play in the construction of that ideology? Is film simply a reflection of ideology or does it create ideology? Do we expect black men to take up an American ideology when that ideology is steeped in oppression? It would simply be too uncritical to dismiss film as entertainment, distraction, or incidental to the creation of ideology. Filmmakers, in their portrayals of black male masculinity, and what they see as its good and evil aspects, certainly do not.

Notions of masculinity have been socially constructed, historically specific, and mediated by social class, race, ethnicity, and other social categories of inequality. Historically, filmmakers and directors have made the decision to assign the role of deviant or "Other" to men of color in the construction of a masculine ideology that is largely confined to a white monolithic ideal.[174] The result has been to not only represent blackness, but to represent black heterosexual maleness as the polar opposite to white heterosexual maleness.[175] Thus, to prove their masculinity black men must be promiscuous, brutish, or deviant, less they be labeled gay, and thus, feminine. The empty representational space allows for and rewards the conflation of masculinity with sexuality. One cannot be a real man unless and until "you bang some hoes." Gay men are then forever cast out of real manliness.

Black masculinity is represented in films at the extremes. Most images portray hyper-success or hyper-deviance.[176] Black men, therefore, are both the embodiment of American success and the symbol of American deviance.[177] This is not to suggest that black men are limited to one stereotype or that black men are simply represented as being in one social or economic tier. It is to suggest that despite the fact that black men are shown in different roles and stations of life in films, the prevailing image of blackness as something loathsome, marginal, and deviant—the criminal black man—still persists. In addition to the ar-

---

[174] Guerrero, "The Black Man on Our Screens."

[175] A complete discussion about black male masculinity and heteronormative cinematic representation is beyond the scope of this edition. I do think it important, however, to mention that the dominant portrayal of black men in film has been that of presumed heterosexuals. I will argue that this portrayal in fact is part of the binary construction problem.

[176] Katheryn K. Russell, *The Color of Crime: Racial Hoaxes, White Fear, Black Protectionism, Police Harassment, and Other Macroaggressions* (New York: New York University Press, 1997).

[177] See generally, *Ethnic Notions: Black Images in the White Mind*, Exhibition, Berkley Art Center, 1982; *Black History: Lost, Stolen or Strayed*, CBS News, CBS, 1968; *A Century of Black Cinema*, Passport Video, 1977; *Bamboozled*, Spike Lee New Line Productions, 2000; and the works of Oscar Micheaux, Clarence Muse, and other black filmmakers.

chetypical criminal, the black man has also been portrayed as a hyper-sexual brute with an insatiable lust for white women.

Emancipation was instrumental in the construction of the "buck" that is the black rapist. Thus, the black bucks of films are psycho-paths—one always panting and salivating, the other forever stiffening his body, as if the mere presence of a white woman in the same room could bring him to a sexual climax. Griffith played hard on the beastial-ity of his black villainous bucks and used it to arouse hatred.[178]

The movie *King Kong*, renamed *King Kong and the White Woman*, brought the hypersexual, animalistic black man and his insatiable appe-tite for white women to the screen.[179] Consider the visual of the big black ape, beating his chest and clutching the petite, blond white wom-an as if she were a trophy or the spoils of war and he the victor to whom the spoils rightly belonged. Arguing that "in all Hollywood film portrayals of blacks [...] the political is never far from the sexual,"[180] Snead links the image of King Kong rampaging through the streets of Manhattan with a defenseless white woman clutched to his body to the increasing economic emasculation of white men in the Depression years, and the growing fear that black migration from the South had reduced the number of jobs available to working-class whites. King Kong's death at the end of the movie remasculinizes the white man, not only because he conquers the black menace, but he also regains the woman. In this way, representations of black men and white men are not isolated images working independently, but rather "correlate [...] in a larger scheme of semiotic valuation."[181] Thus, the image of the black male as sexual savage serves to construct white male sexuality as the protector of white womanhood, as contained, and importantly, as capable of intimacy and humanity. As with the justification of the buck

---

[178] Donald Bogle, *Toms, Coons, Mulattoes, Mammies, and Bucks*, (New York: Viking Press, 1973) 13.

[179] Guerrero, "The Black Man on Our Screens," 399.

[180] J. Snead, *White Screen, Black Images: Hollywood from the Dark Side* (New York: Routledge, 1994) 8.

[181] Snead 9.

stereotype, this movie capitalized on the growing fear of working-class whites to the black migration to northern cities.

In March 2008, Vogue Magazine and photographer Annie Leibiovitz revived the King Kong image in a racially unapologetic way. Vogue was proud to announce that LeBron James of the Cleveland Cavaliers was the first black man to grace its cover. On the cover, James clutched a white woman model, Gisele Bundchen, as he growled and snarled in a pose mocking the menacing face of a guerilla. One wonders why Vogue did not simply supply him with a guerilla suit and a banana. This would have completed the caricature and revived notions of King Kong. Vogue, its editors, James, Lebovitiz, and Bundchen either did not understand the depth of the imagery or did not care. Their motivation or knowledge is besides the point. It proves that the film purveyed the image, media supported it, and America buys it. James enacted his agency to do just what was expected, claim his black male masculinity. Of course, in the days of anti-miscegenation laws, that portrayal would not have been allowed and James and his accomplices would have been jailed.

FILM AND LAW

Film and law have historically colluded to create and reinforce the perception that white women need to be protected from the created image of black male masculinity. The antimiscegenation laws served as a powerful tool, and appeared in the statutes of almost every state until they were struck down by the United States Supreme Court in 1967.[182] King Kong sent a powerful message to lawmakers: Protect white women from deviant black male masculinity at all costs. The not so subtle subtext was that there was a need to regulate black male sexuality in general, but particularly as it related to their interactions with white women. The message was that black male sexuality and masculinity is one in the same. Never mind that this conflation was a creature of filmmakers. Film had served its purpose of defining black male sexuality, exposing its dangers, tying it exclusively to sex acts, and demanding its regulation. Anti-miscegenation laws were intended to re-

---

[182] Loving v. Virginia, 388 U.S. 1. See generally Robert J. Sickels, *Race, Marriage, and the Law* (Albuquerque: University of New Mexico Press, 1972).

spond to the hue and cry of film. These laws made it a crime for black men to marry white women. In many cases, law enforcement would barge into the marital bedrooms of interracial couples and arrest them for having married.

The states generally claimed that these laws were simply intended to separate the races. The reality, however, is that these laws acted to prevent the brutish black man from soiling the pure white woman. The intent of these laws was to prevent the intermixture of the races so that the morphological differences that code as race could be more neatly maintained.[183] The courts and the states established the laws and the filmmakers distributed them and defined the legal and social relationships articulated by them to the masses via the silver screen.

Slavery created and maintained the subordination of black people. Stereotypical representations of the black male during slavery defined black male masculinity. Thus, representations of black men in film cannot be viewed as simply a filmmaker's prejudice or point of view, but must be considered through the triple vectors of law, mainstream history, and culture. Moreover, any discussion of race and film must take into account its global reality, since America not only exports film, it also exports its notion of black male masculinity.

Birth of a Nation, a film that was widely regarded as a significant American cinematic success, fused the two most basic racial themes of the Jim Crow South, demonstrating the symbiotic and codependent relationship between the minstrel show and lynching. In the latter case, it reinforced the widely accepted image of black men as beasts who lusted after innocent white women and girls, and whose uncontrollable sexual deviances and desires controlled their lives. *Birth of a Nation* made clear that the innocent white women and girls were so repulsed by this seemingly innate sexual deviance that they would rather jump off a cliff to their deaths than be ravaged, and therefore soiled for life, by the base, vile animal that was the black man.

This representation of black men was attacked by many as negative stereotyping. Thus, there was a need to counter negative portrayals with

---

[183] See Virginia Dominguez, *White by Definition: Social Classification in Creole Louisiana* (New Brunswick: Rutgers University Press, 1986); Paul Finkleman, "The Crime of Color," *Tul. L. Rev.* 67 (1993): 2063, 2081-87.

positive portrayals. It would, therefore, be inaccurate to suggest that the portrayal of the black man has been limited to Sambo, animals, or black brutes. In fact, film has given us Sidney Poitier as the "perfect" black man in *Guess Whose Coming to Dinner?*, Melvin Van Peebles as sexually rebellious in *Sweetback and* "Mister" in *The Color Purple*, and the thugged out gangstas with their harem of "bitches and hos," most notoriously 50 Cent in *Get Rich or Die Tryin'*. And some critics have told us that we should be pleased by the progressive portrayals of the black man as represented by the buffoonery of Ludricas, and the conflicted black man in the person of Terrance Howard in *CRASH*. The representational empty space, it seems, continues albeit in different forms.

CHAPTER TWELVE
TELEVISION

Although this edition focuses on the big screen, I think it is critical to mention that the small screen (television) has also played an important role in constructing and portraying black men for mass consumption. On television, we were presented with the idyllic Bill Cosby as Cliff Huckstable, as well as the nameless "black suspect" on the 6'oclock news, who could have been any black man, anywhere, anytime. Eddie Murphy reintroduced "Buckwheat," The Wyanans gave us "Men on Film," and there was "Good Times" and George Jefferson. Television's representations were not only limited to comedy, drama, and other genres; true to the supposed neutrality of "reporting the news" we were inundated with images of the animalistic treatment of Rodney King, the representation of miscegenation in the trial of O. J. Simpson, and the actualized brute as portrayed by Mike Tyson. As Sly Stallone of *Rocky* fame has said, there is a wisdom and profit in loving and hating black men. The black man is portrayed through a cultural lens that is fundamentally focused on fantasies of sex and violence.

MISSISSIPPI BURNING

Television has also treated us to shows such as *Mississippi Burning*. *Mississippi Burning* arrived in 1998 to mixed reviews from various quarters. Pauline Keal of *The New Yorker* wrote:

> Parker used the civil rights movement to make a Charles Bronson movie, and from his blithe public statements, he seems unaware that this could be morally repugnant. [...] The manipu-

lation got to me all right, but the only emotion I felt was hatred for the movie.[184]

Roger Ebert, on the other hand, called it "the best American movie of the year"[185] and stated that it is one of the only movies he had ever seen that showed the real passion of race relations in America, a topic generally too taboo to discuss.

Major criticisms of the movie included that it used gratuitous violence to dramatize the deaths of the civil rights workers, exaggerated the extent of racism in the South, and that it was designed to condition the audience to expect brutality whenever a black person came into a scene. Thus, a sampling of reviews at the time suggested that it was the intent of the filmmaker to cause viewers to hate the Klan and pity the blacks. This criticism is collusive, privileged, and just another example of how whites in America often see race through the rear view mirror. As a group, while whites are affected by race, they can simply view race, have the privilege of critiquing race, while living privileged because of their race.

I will argue that for all of its limitations, *Mississippi Burning* added to the discourse on race, and that attempts to dismiss it as overly violent miss the point. In the context of the civil rights struggles portrayed in the movie, racism was by definition violent. To portray it as otherwise would be to rewrite the history of racism in a way that may have assuaged white guilt while trivializing the fact that blatant racism survived for as long as it did not in spite of violence but because of it.

OLE' MIS'

The opening sequence skillfully and deliberately frames the movie. It becomes clear that the director intends to use fire as a metaphor for hatred, oppression, destruction, and racism. Images of the burning houses, the burning crosses, and the fire bombings are indelibly etched into the viewer's mind throughout the film. The slow, deliberate, and unnerving long shot of the car through the pitch dark of the night, coupled with the soundtrack which seems to be in lockstep with the

---

[184] Jim Emerson, *Mississippi Burning* (1988), 10 May 2008 <http://cinepad.com/reviews/mississippi.htm> par. 5.

[185] Emerson par. 4.

Klansmen as they march towards murder, does in fact construct the hatred that viewers are conditioned to feel for the Klansmen and their supporters throughout the movie. It also serves to produce empathy for the civil rights workers and to argue for the work of civil rights.

With speed and music as a weapon, the threat becomes obvious and the camera takes us out of our seats and places us in the car. The director makes clear that it is the black activist who understands the depth and breath of the danger when he says, "Oh they ain't playing, you better believe me." We have moved from the establishing long shot of the car to terrifying close-ups framing the head and chin of one of the Klansmen, whose paunch, gait, and disposition lets us know that he is judge, jury, and executioner. The director effectively uses several high-angle shots to establish the dominant and oppressive nature of the law (as represented by the police) and the oppressed and subjugated nature of the civil rights workers. Moreover, these high-angle shots also establish that civil rights have been subjugated by the power of the law.

Given what the director is trying to establish, violence is not incidental to the film; it is central to the film. The Klan was not simply a group of people who got together and discussed how best to establish racists policy through mediation and dialogue. They were, by nature, and in their view necessarily, a group who used violence and were an extension of the law. They fought intervention by the federal government, because as one of the Klansmen so eloquently explained in the movie "our niggers were happy until y'all got here." So, how then can a movie about violence be devoid of violence? How can a movie about cross burning and fire bombing not show cross burning and fire bombing? Racism in Mississippi at the time depicted in the film was not simply ideological, it was violent. Racism was practiced through the barrel of a gun, the knot of a noose, and the complicity of the law. Therefore, it is inaccurate to dismiss the film because it used graphic, violent imagery to make its point. The film did not create racist violence; it simply tried to illustrate it for viewers. To do otherwise would have left viewers looking at race through a rear view mirror—from a comfortable distance, unless of course you are black.

THE ARTICULATION OF RACE

The film articulates race in ways that might be expected. Among them: the pathological victimology of blacks which requires a benevolent white male savior, and the white woman who is not really racist but has been told it enough to believe it. However, civil rights for blacks were a largely theoretical concept at the time period in which this movie is set, so it would not be unusual for blacks to be both victims and repeatedly subject to victimization. Moreover, at that time, the FBI was overwhelmingly white and male; thus, it would not have been unusual for the agents to be both white and male. The struggle between the liberal white male and the more conservative white male seems to be "resolved" at the end of the film. Using wide-angle shots of Ward and Anderson leaving, the camera pans the landscape of the cemetery and finally comes to rest not on a person, but on the date on the smashed tombstone—1964.

To some, this suggests that the film was more about the white men and less about everyone else. Given that the film was intended for a white, liberal audience, this should not surprise anyone. The director made the film to persuade a white liberal audience of the ills of racism. To do so, he had to lift up and sell the tropes of white male bravado and conversion to what is right. What is right, in the director's view, is to fight for civil rights at all cost, facts be damned. The fact is that the FBI, under J. Edgar Hoover, did not care about the rights of blacks and did what it could to violate those rights. This attempt to revise history not only ignores facts, it creates them. The problem with this recreation of history is that it continues to marginalize blacks and privilege whites.

> That anyone can purport to do a film about Mississippi in 1964 and push Blacks to the sidelines and make the FBI the heroes can only be understood if this film is viewed through the prism of the reactionary cultural mores of the 1980s [and '90s], particularly the clear emergence of an anti-democratic trend in U.S. popular culture. Part of this process has been the resur-

gence of racism in the arts and a whitening of roles and themes.[186]

The biggest problem with the movie was its attempt to ignore the fact that the FBI was an institution based on racism and its attempt to recast it as the benevolent savior. The truth of the FBI's long investigation in Neshoba County was that it was neither very efficient, nor, in the end, particularly dramatic. In the film, the key revelation in the case comes when Mr. Hackman, at once courtly and cynical, uses seduction as a means of obtaining information. The reality is less romantic. The actual "seduction" was a $30,000 FBI payoff to a Klan informant. *Mississippi Burning* (1988) is bad history, because the dramatic inventions it uses violate the consensus of historical scholarship on Freedom Summer 1964. The film gives a pair of fictional FBI agent's credit for protecting African-Americans and advancing civil rights, when in fact the FBI only belatedly and reluctantly became involved.

> Dorothy Zellner, a white southerner who took part in Freedom Summer in 1964, summed up the negative assessment about this film, held by a lot of activists, when she noted: The real problem is that it distorts the basic fact of the civil rights movement: that Black people, in an electric moment in history, organized hundreds of thousands of people in the U.S. to obtain elementary civil rights for everyone. Responding to such criticism Parke, the film's director said: Our film isn't about the civil rights movement. It's about why there was a need for a civil rights movement. And because it's a movie I felt it had to be fictionalized. The two heroes in the story had to be white. That is a reflection of our society as much as of the film industry. At this point in time, it could not have been made any other way.[187]

Race has been created, articulated, and rearticulated through film. Film, like so many forms of entertainment has the power to inform, entertain, and shape perceptions of race and racism. It also has the

---

[186] Frances M. Beal, "Warped Lens Distorts Mississippi Burning," 27 Feb. 1989, *Frontline*, 10 May 2008 <http://www.hartford-hwp.com/ archives/45a/453.html> par. 6.

[187] Beal par. 4.

power to reinforce that which we bring to film. Film is often critiqued as if viewers are blank slates passively waiting to be brainwashed by the omnipotent power of film. It is clear that we come to film with our own predispositions on issues of race, gender, and related topics; thus, film in many cases is the filter through which we see life and/or our own experiences. Film may make us feel comfortable with ourselves and our views on race. Conversely, it may make some people uncomfortable, because they feel guilty about something that is exposed. The oft-leveled criticism of *Mississippi Burning* is that it was too violent and therefore not relevant. However, perhaps that criticism is raised because to admit that racism was that violent would require whites, who considered themselves "liberal, anti-racists" or "pacifists," to have to ask whether they could see themselves in the film.

CHAPTER THIRTEEN
FILM AS A LEGAL LENS

I have provided an explication of the portrayal of black men in film and concluded that the representations presented by the industry are extreme and provide an infantile and incomplete picture of black men. Our society is in need of a mature, multi-dimensional representation of black men that is not constrained by the current positive-negative binaries. I begin this section with a historical perspective of the law, the racialization of the black man, and his subsequent portrayal in film. I then turn to an analysis of emancipation, civil rights, and post-civil rights portrayals. Next, I provide a modern analysis of the black male portrayal and I conclude with a paradigm for portraying the black man through film.

> In America, black people were portrayed as inferior almost from their time of enslavement in the colonies in the 1620s. This racial characterization enabled white masters to justify slavery as something positive. Using racial stereotypes to justify the enslavement of blacks was especially pronounced after 1830 as white Southerners defended slavery against attacks by northern abolitionists.[188]

Discussions about race and racism in America, as well as about slavery, often involve comparing the North and the South. The "Great Liberals" of the North established tools to ensure that at least formally, slavery had been taken off the books by 1830. While northern blacks were arguably treated "better" than southern blacks; they were still

---

[188] Davis par. 2.

treated as patently unequal and were still living in communities that were racially segregated. For all of their liberal leanings, northern whites still saw themselves as superior, although not as barbaric as their southern brethren. Abraham Lincoln put it best "there must be the position of superior and inferior, and I as much as any other man am in favor of having the superior position assigned to the white race."[189]

> By the eve of the Civil War the North had sharply defined its position on white supremacy: Negro subordination, and racial segregation. The political party that took control of the federal government at that time was in accord with this position, and Abraham Lincoln as its foremost spokesperson was on record with repeated endorsements.[190]

Constructing and articulating race and racial categories was not limited to the South. It was, and still is, an American tool. Constructing race and sustaining its articulation required more than ideology; it required imagery. The imagery would have to depict blacks in a way that could justify continuing racial subordination. The imagery would have to be such that law would have a basis to legally justify the subordination while appearing to issue neutral and detached reasoning. Imagery, ideology, and law would collude to intellectualize and justify black subordination. The images included the cover of Helen Bannerman's *Little Black Sambo*. Despite Bannerman setting the story in India, the racist iconography was unmistakable. The illustrations in the original European version portrayed Sambo as having skin as black as tar and lips as red as cherries. Sambo was used to describe the archetypal black buffoon who would reinforce the existing stereotypes of blacks that were held by many whites. His job was to make whites laugh at his black chicanery. The Sambo image was also highly gendered, such that one would never imagine Sambo to be anything other than a boy. Thus, Sambo as a proxy for all black men in America was powerful. To whites, Sambo would always be a boy, just like black men, no matter how old they were would always be boys. In addition to Sambo, there was Jiggaboo, an extremely dark-skinned black person with big lips, a wide nose, and nappy hair. The Jiggaboo image was widely purveyed in cartoons, newspaper images and other media of the time as being "authentically black." There was also the mooncricket, which was used to describe blacks who would only come out at night and sing slave songs as a cricket chirped under the moonlight. The mooncricket image

[189] Abraham Lincoln, *The Collected Works of Abraham Lincoln,* eds. Roy Basler, Marion Dolores Pratt, and Lloyd A. Dunlap (New Brunswick, NJ: Rutgers University Press, 1953–55) 1064.

[190] Woodward 21.

was critical in that it reinforced the stereotypes of blacks as musical and also laid the foundation for the popular stereotype that dark-skinned blacks can only be seen when they smile. (Envision a cricket with a large white smile.) Uncle Tom, of course, was used to refer to the black man whose job it was to "sell out" his people and himself for the acceptance of whites. The Uncle Tom image was critical for whites who wanted to believe that there were some good blacks who knew their place and that by knowing their place, they would not threaten the physical security of whites.

The Tom caricature portrays black men as faithful, happily submissive servants. The Tom caricature, as with the Mammy caricature, was born in antebellum America in the defense of slavery. How could slavery be wrong, argued its proponents, if black servants, males (Toms) and females (Mammies) were contented, loyal servants? The Tom is presented as a smiling, wide-eyed, dark-skinned server: fieldworker, cook, butler, porter, or waiter. Unlike the Coon, the Tom is portrayed as a dependable worker, eager to serve. Unlike the brute, the Tom is docile and non-threatening to whites. The Tom is often old, physically weak, psychologically dependent on whites for approval.[191] All of these and many more images were purveyed by whites as a way of establishing blacks as permanent and hopeless caricatures deserving of vile, debasing treatment.

The caricatures were soon used by advertisers. In 1892, Arbuckle Brothers Coffee produced trading cards depicting "darkies" picking cotton on the right, and a map of Alabama on the left. In 1892 Arbuckle's trading cards depicted "darkies" picking cotton together with a Civil War scene. There were also advertisements promoting minstrel shows produced in 1900 by the Strobridge Lithograph Company in which a black man, who was portrayed as fat and lazy, brandished a gun to protect his watermelon patch while pickininnies tried to steal his melons.

And so, the stage was set. America had defined blacks through a series of stereotypes that would be used by the courts as they determined the ambit of protection that the law would give blacks. Since the United States courts were operating in a civil rights context, the white male judges would have unfettered discretion to use racial stereotypes, both those they held personally and those that dominated the media, as the basis for their decisions. The fact that they donned the black robes

---

[191] "The Tom Caricature," *Jim Crow: Museum of Racist Memorabilia*, Ferris State University, 10 May 2008 <http://www.ferris.edu/ jim-crow/tom/>.

to dispense "blind justice" did not mean that they as white judges could or would let go of their whiteness and its attendant racism.

> However real and monstrous this burden, it is important to remember that the entire purpose of the social construction we call race, is and always has been, to serve the interests of those deemed White, to create the benefits that go along with being deemed White. Slavery gave Whites a labor force to which they owed nothing and from which they might demand anything. Apartheid provided Whites with a formal structure that facilitated the unequal distribution of the state's wealth and favor, all during a period of our history that still carries the ironic label "separate but equal." Contemporary racism, the legacy of our past, like apartheid and slavery before it, provides Whites with an intangible but powerful sense of racial superiority. When, for example, we entertain the assumption that Blacks generally speaking, are not hard-working, we are always implicitly proclaiming the industriousness of Whites. Every place that excludes Blacks becomes a place Whites are presumably welcome. The cumulative effect of all this racism is that Whites emerge with a presumptive sense of worthiness and belonging.[192]

In this quote, Ross exposes what white judges faced, but chose to ignore in making landmark civil rights rulings in the United States. How could they present objective and detached rulings on race when they believed the caricatures that came to represent blackness? Since the law constructed race in a way that was advantageous to whites at the expense of blacks, wouldn't it be counterintuitive to rule against these doctrinal precepts? As active and willing participants in creating and rearticulating the story of race in America, could American judges render any decision that would recognize how racism impacted the lives of blacks? We would soon find answers in an emerging American racial jurisprudence.

> An extraordinary number of rationales surfaced as criteria in the prerequisite decisions. However, in the complex task of racial definition, judges deciding prerequisite cases relied primarily on four distinct rationales: (1) common knowledge, (2)

---

[192] Thomas Ross, "The Unbearable Whiteness of Being," *Crossroads, Directions, and a New Critical Race Theory,* eds. Francisco Valdes, Jerome McCristal Culp, and Angela P. Harris (Philadelphia: Tempe University Press, 2002) 253–254.

scientific evidence, (3) congressional intent, and (4) legal precedent. [193]

Judges, whether acting through the vectors of common knowledge, scientific evidence, congressional intent, or legal precedent could not separate the myth of black racial inferiority from judicial reasoning and analysis. The NAACP's civil rights chickens had come home to roost.

As law was asserting itself as a regulatory powerhouse, film was asserting itself as a cultural powerhouse. According to Brownlow:

> Numerically dominated by males, these immigrant assemblages exhibited in their recreational habits what polite society ascribed as the vices of the ignorant poor: alcoholism, drugs (ranging from cigarettes to opium), and rowdy combativeness. In order to relieve the sexual frustrations and loneliness which resulted from the separation from their families and native communities, their overt sexual impulses fostered prostitution and the transformation of the cheap burlesque theater into female exhibitionism. And by 1910, it was discovered they constituted three quarters of the 26 million who made up the movie audience. [194]

Social and high-culture creator Mary Grey Peck of the Women's Club put it this way: "Motion pictures are going to save our civilization from the destruction which has successfully overwhelmed every civilization in the past. They provide what every previous civilization has lacked—namely a means of relief, happiness and mental inspiration for people at the bottom."[195] So film was not only for entertainment, it was also designed to save American civilization from extinction and disappearing into the cultural abyss.

It became the role of the law to set up proper relationships between the races in American society. In so doing, it determined who was white, and thus entitled to respect and dignity, and who was black, and thus little more than chattel to be bought, sold, bartered, denigrated, and

---

[193] Lopez 63.

[194] K. Brownlow, *Behind the Mask of Innocence,* (Berkley: University of California, 1990) 233–234.

[195] Mary Gray Peck, speech, the General Federation of Women's Clubs, 1917.

demonized. Law was also making clear that there was a dominant male ideal. That ideal said that in order to be a man in American society, one would of course have to first be born male. However, maleness was not the only social construction that mattered. One had to be both male and white. So, while black men may have been privileged by their gender in a male dominated society, they were subsequently oppressed by the law based on their race;. The law did not consider them white men; thus, they were not "real" men within the white dominant ideology.

The relationship between law and film was therefore crystallized. The role of law was to define social and legal relationships and the role of film was to package and distribute that role for all to see. Since film was becoming such an important cultural vehicle, it would work hand in hand with law to transmit cultural messages about the relationships, stereotypes, and constructions defined by law to the masses via the power of the silver screen.

As a matter of course, there is an inextricable link between the powerful institutions of law and film in the creation and representation of black men in America. It is clear that the development of law and film in the United States has created a cultural arena that is highly racialized, so neither can be examined from an ostensibly neutral perspective. Thus, the symbiotic and codependent relationship between the two has been integral in furthering the way Americans, both black and white, imagine themselves to be part of a nation specifically favored by whiteness. Having established the relationship between law and film, I turn now to an examination of black male representation during emancipation and reconstruction.

CHAPTER FOURTEEN
EMANCIPATION, RECONSTRUCTION, AND MISREPRESENTATION

An important characteristic of a stereotype is that it is often an image which is shared by those who hold a common cultural mindset—it is representative of the way a culture or significant sub-group within that culture, defines and labels a specific group of people.[196] Filmmakers[197] created the stereotype of the 'buck' and used it as shorthand for the black rapist. Early forms of entertainment, such as film[198] and vaudeville shows propagandized the buck image to further demonize black male masculinity. The buck was indelibly etched into the nation's collective and cultural consciousness and is a cinematic image which

---

[196] Jack Nachbar and Kevin Lause, *Popular Culture* (Bowling Green: University Popular Press, 1992).

[197] From 1908 to 1914, motion picture production and exhibition had been dominated by Edison's cartel, the Motion Picture Patents Company ('The Trust', as Carl Lamelle termed it). The Trust included Edison, Biograph, Vitagraph, Essanay, Kalem, Selig, Lubin, Pathe Freres, Melies, and George Kliene. The members of the near-monopoly—based on the patents for cameras, projectors, etc., which were held by Edison's company, American Mutoscope, and Biograph—were primarily older, white Anglo-Saxton Protestants who had entered the film industry in its infancy by inventing, bankrolling, or tinkering with movie hardware. See, generally, R. Sklar, *Movie Made America* (New York: Random House, 1975).

[198] In 1908, *The World Today* declared that pictures were "the academy of the working man, his pulpit, his newspaper club."

persists to the present day.[199] The representation and cinematic oppression of black men in film is nothing new; it is as old as America itself.[200]

The film that played a significant role in the creation and nurturing of the black man on film is *Birth of a Nation.* Lauded for its cinematic prowess, yet pilloried for its visual lynching and castration of the black man, *Birth of a Nation* remains "an uneasy presence in American film history."[201] Upon its release, *Birth* was advertised as a film that would "work audiences into a frenzy [...] it will make you hate."[202]

The black male characters to hate in *Birth* were Gus, a black man played by a white man in blackface[203] and Silas Lynch[204]. Gus is to be hated for his pursuit and threatened rape of Flora, which Griffith implies leads to her decision to commit suicide rather than be defiled by Gus. In fact, her family, in mourning her death, made it clear that her decision to jump to her death was based on honor. According to the movie, "for her who had learned the stern lesson of honor, we should not grieve that she found sweeter the opal gates of death."

Lynch is also to be hated for his pursuit of Elsie, a white woman whom Lynch attempts to force marriage upon. Elsie threatens him with

---

[199] Bogle.

[200] Brownlow, a filmmaker and historian of the silent era, indicated that the period between 1919 was the "richest source of social films."

[201] Fred Silva, ed., *Focus on Birth of a Nation* (Englewood Cliffs, N.J.: Prentice-Hall, 1971) 1–2.

[202] Bogle 11–12.

[203] Michael Rogin observed that "Griffith's Negros [sic] were as bad as he painted them because he painted whites black [...] Griffith allowed a few blacks to act the nigger. But he did not want to let the representation of blackness go." M. Rogin, "The Sword Became a Flashing Vision," D. W. Griffith, ed., "The Birth of a Nation," *Representations* 9 (Winter, 1985) 150–195.

[204] Here again, film and law intersect. Lynch is of mixed racial heritage, but the one-drop rule is in effect, so he is, for all intents and purposes, a black man.

a "horsewhipping for his insolence." Lusting for power and miscegenation, his intention is to marry her, by force if necessary.

Through his carefully constructed fusion of unprecedented technical wizardry and degrading racial stereotypes, D. W. Griffith sought to convince this audience that his was the 'true' story of the old South and that white domination was necessary for their survival. To a great extent, he succeeded; the film's enormous popularity fueled the growing influence of the Klan and *Birth of a Nation* remains to this day one of the highest grossing box office successes in Hollywood history.[205]

Thus, the film is an important line of demarcation in the portrayal of the black man as the baseless black rapist in constant pursuit of the white woman who both film and law has constructed as fragile, pure, and virginal. The law made it clear that the races were to be placed into the binary of purity (whiteness) and vulgarity (blackness). *Birth of a Nation* is instructive in that it produced, directed, and distributed the black man to the masses as little more than a disembodied penis constantly aroused whenever a white woman, any white woman, would come in contact with it. While the buck was the dominant portrayal of black men during this period, Coon, Sambo, Uncle Tom, and the brute were also images of black men that were prevalent in popular American culture and so found their way into film as well. The result of these portrayals is what Professor Russell labels "the dominant gaze."

I would like to suggest three distinct ways in which the dominant gaze functions: (1) in the proliferation of degrading stereotypes which serves to dehumanize blacks' history, lives and experiences; (2) in the marginalization or complete absence of indigenous perspectives on blacks' history, lives and experiences; and (3) in the co-optation or Hollywood-ization of ostensibly 'racial themes' to capitalize on the perceived trendiness or fashionableness of such perspectives.[206]

---

[205] Bogle 11–12.

[206] Margaret M. Russell, "Race and the Dominant Gaze: Narratives of Law and Inequality in Popular Film," *Legal Studies Forum* 15.3 (1991): 246.

With the dominant gaze as their backdrop, both Hollywood and independent filmmakers felt the need to respond to the proliferation of negative stereotypes of black men in film. As a result, the dominant gaze produced Lena Horne and Eddie (Rochester) Anderson in *Cabin in The Sky,* and Horne and Bill Robinson in *Stormy Weather.* The dominant gaze was also responsible for Sidney Poitier, Harry Belafonte, and Sammy Davis Jr., who were thrust into leading-men roles. While all of these roles had their share of critics and supporters, Poitier's role in *Guess Whose Coming to Dinner?* was, in my view, a white liberal, integrationist view of the black man. That is, Poitier was no longer the buck dominated by his penis in the quest for the white woman. In fact, the movie portrayed the couple as asexual. He was instead, a new and improved version of the black man who was educated, professional, and without sexual desire. He was, in a word, the "acceptable" Negro. The problem, however, with this "positive" portrayal of the black man was that it was still steeped in the dominant gaze. He was represented as the exception to the rule. Hollywood had invented "the perfect Negro" while at the same time making clear that even his perfection did not mean that his credentials would not be questioned.[207]

The problem with this portrayal is that it was a vacuous, hypersanitized, anemic, one-dimensional portrayal of a black man. It was no different than a brute, a buck, Sambo, or Gus, except that it was not based in penis superiority and vaudeville buffoonery. So, while Hollywood tried to move away from the negative stereotype of the black man, it did so in a way that simply created a new one. Hollywood was still trapped by the dominant gaze. Moreover, it was also clear that while times were changing, Hollywood's investment in whiteness, which was aided and abetted by the law, was still influenced by the legacy of slavery and segregation, which was endemic in America. As Richard Dyer suggests, "[W]hite power secures its dominance by seeming not to be anything in particular."[208] "As the unmarked category

---

[207] In the film, the fact that Poitier's character was a doctor had to be verified by a member of the clergy. This was a not too subtle message that as acceptable a Negro as he was, there was still a need for a white man to vouch for him. The message is clear—you are at the door, not in the door.

[208] Richard Dyer, "White," *Screen* 29.4 (1988): 44.

against which the difference is constructed, whiteness never has to speak its name, never has to acknowledge its role as an organizing principle in social and cultural relations."[209]

---

[209] Chandra Mukerji and Michael Schudson, eds., introduction, *Rethinking Popular Culture: Contemporary Perspectives in Cultural Studies* (Berkley: University of California Press, 1991) **page.

CHAPTER FIFTEEN
THE CIVIL RIGHTS MOVEMENT AND THE BLACK MAN

The fight to convert Hollywood began in the '60s during the civil rights movement. It was a time during which the redefinition of the black experience was aggressively addressed and Sidney Poitier had established himself as the only black actor to work consistently in leading dramatic roles. Although the Academy Award winner made his mark on the decade, he was viewed as a rather chaste character until 1968.[210]

During the 1960s, America was starting to experience the civil rights movement as both legal and cultural phenomena. Given the primacy of film in facilitating this experience, films portraying the black man began to take on a harsher, more politically-demanding edge. These films, both from abroad and later from outside the major studios, challenged the simplistic optimism of Poitier's heyday.[211]

> Costa-Gavras' *The Battle of Algiers* (1966) seemed to some black militants a textbook for direct action, while Amiri Baraka spoke of the movie version of his short play *Dutchman* (1967) as a "revolutionary revelation." Even Hollywood's

---

[210] Walter Leavy, "50 Years of Black Love in Movies – Special 50th Anniversary Feature," Ebony (Feb 1995), 10 May 2008 <http://findarticles.com/p/articles/mi_m1077/is_n4_v50/ai_16412385> par. 10.

[211] "Blacks in American Film," *AfricanAmericans.com,* 10 May 2008 <http://www.africanamericans.com/Films.htm> par. 19.

movies hardened. Robert Mulligan's film version of Harper Lee's novel *To Kill a Mockingbird* (1962) ended with the death of its black protagonist, and Sidney Lumet's *The Pawnbroker* (1965) was set in harsh Harlem and dominated by a coldly ominous drug dealer (played by Brock Peters). By way of contrast, more pastoral films such as Martin Ritt's *Sounder* (1972) and Gordon Parks's autobiographical *The Learning Tree* (1969) seemed childlike in their remoteness from the coming wave of angry films.[212]

"Catalysts for this turn toward rage were the cities of the late 1960s that burst into riots of despair at the assassination of Martin Luther King Jr. and what appeared to be the exhaustion of his movement."[213] The civil rights movement and its aftermath created separate living and movie viewing space. But, how would that living and movie space be used? Who would use it? To what end? Would the post civil rights era vindicate or indict the civil rights movement? Who owned the images? How would those images be controlled and by whom? Would those images be contested and non-specific? Would black youths of successive generations even care about the movement?

"The prototype of the new genre, soon dubbed 'Blaxploitation' films by the trade paper Variety, was Melvin Van Peeble's *Sweet Sweetback's Baadasssss Song* (1971)."[214] *Sweetback* was made at the height of the male-dominated black power rebellion and so its dismissive and crude black macho male view of the black woman was no surprise. "*Sweetback* marked a representational turning point for the black male image on the big screen."[215] *Sweetback* provided the black audience with a counter to the sappy, want-to-be-white, uppity Negro that was often offered up by Poitier. Drawn on the "bad nigger" archetype in African-American folklore, the sexual rebel and outlaw Sweetback, battles whitey without relenting. Because of its independent "guerilla

---

[212] "Blacks in American Film," par. 19.

[213] "Blacks in American Film," par. 20.

[214] "Blacks in American Film," par. 20.

[215] Ed Guerrero, *Framing Blackness: The African American Image in Film* (Philadelphia: Temple University Press, 1993).

financing: manifesto and the aesthetic, gender, and political debates
that it still inspires, *Sweetback* stands as a vital marker in the discourse
about the construction of black manhood."[216]

> If *Birth of a Nation* was the white man's creation of a black
> man, *Sweetback* was the black man's revenge. More than any
> other movie, *Sweetback* defined its era. Soulful and provoca-
> tive with its lighting and sound track, and heady with contempt
> for the white social order and its cops, the film's success all
> but invited Hollywood's major studios to rush forward in pur-
> suit of the new audience. MGM's *Shaft* (1971), for example,
> created an ass-kicking, macho, heterosexual, black streetwise
> hero who, in reality, was not an outlaw in Sweetback's mold,
> but merely a plainclothes cop. From the outset, the Hollywood
> studio version of this black, urban, outlaw culture cynically
> followed familiar patterns. *Cool Breeze* (1972) was remade
> from *The Asphalt Jungle*, *The Lost Man* (1969) from Carol
> Reed's *Odd Man Out*, and *Up Tight* (1968) from John Ford's
> film of an Irish rebellion, *The Informer*. The Hollywood stu-
> dios even plundered horror movies and created films such as
> *Blacula* (1972) and *Blackenstein* (1972).[217]

The foundations for the binary portrayals of black men were, to a
large extent, poured during the *Birth of a Nation* so "Blaxploitation"
simply built its own black man on that foundation. It did not seek to
correct for the problematic portrayal of the black man; it simply replaced it with another. While Blaxploitation was "black" in cinematic
theory, its portrayals of black men cannot escape critique because of its
"organic" or "counter representational" portrayal of the black man. As
Manthia Diawara puts it,

> I am less interested in the debates over positive and negative
> images. Instead of liberating Aunt Jemima, Stepin Fetchit, and
> other stereotypes from the grip of white fantasy, positive im-
> ages tend to reinforce the immanence of these stereotypes in
> our collective imagination. That is, the instance on positive

---

[216] Guerrero

[217] "Blacks in American Film," par. 20.

images only strengthens the negative stereotypes in both the black and white imagination.[218, 219]

Sweetback and Blaxploitation spurned a number of films that broaden the debate about black male identity and representation on the silver screen. These included *Hollywood Shuffle* (1987), in which Robert Townsend, playing an aspiring actor, struggles with his conscience and dominant cinema's stereotypical expectations, as he ponders whether he too should play the role of the criminal, the pimp, comic, slave, or butler as Hollywood expected the black man to play.

In 1941, commenting on a demeaning and unintelligible line of dialogue written for her as a mammy-ish maid in *Affectionately Yours*, Butterfly McQueen mused that "I never thought that I would have to say a line like that. I had imagined that since I was an intelligent woman I could play any kind of role."[220] McQueen was not simply musing, she had come to the realization that Hollywood had no roles for intelligent black women but had plenty for "Toms, Coons, mulattoes, Mammies and bucks."[221] Even though a long period of time had passed since McQueen's realization, Hollywood's portrayal of the black man was still marked by buffoonery, Tom foolery, and irrelevance. As a direct opposition to this, *Juice* (1992) and *Menace II Society* (1993) explored the black underworld and interrogated the code of the streets.[222]

---

[218] Manthia Diawara, *The Blackface Stereotype*, 1998, 10 May 2008 <www.blackculturalstudies.org> par. 2.

[219] I do not mean to suggest that Blaxploitation engaged exclusively in positive stereotyping. I am suggesting that this decision to offer up an image of the black man specifically designed to counter the white male hegemony which dominated filmic portrayals up to this point suffers from the same over-simplistic and impotent portrayals for which *Birth of a Nation* was so soundly criticized.

[220] Bogle 93.

[221] Bogle 93.

[222] Andrew Hacker, *Two Nations Black and White, Separate, Hostile, Unequal* (New York: Scribner's, 1992) 3–49.

In addition to serving as the same metaphorical "straight jacket" of the previous periods,

> [t]he very same images of black manhood as threat and dread not only work to disturb dominant white representation of black manhood, they also stand in a conflicted relationships with definitions and images of masculinity within blackness, most notably constructions of black masculinity produced by the middle-class wing of the civil rights movement and those produced more recently by black gay men.[223]
>
> One side effect of such depictions is that the continued negotiation of the norm, in which representations of black gay men have long served a crucial function, will become increasingly complex and difficult, necessitating much more critical examination of the process of such negotiation itself.[224]

That is, for all of their claims to offer an alternative to the demonized black man, films such as *Sweetback* and *Shaft* offered one alternative, the alternative of the straight black man. Film in this area marginalized andor rendered invisible black gay men just like Jim Crow and *Birth of a Nation* did to straight black men. The representations of black men produced by this period were no doubt progress; however, they were not yet complete.

The making of *Malcolm X,* a movie that sparked controversy from the moment of its inception, became a personal mission for Spike Lee who decided to address head-on the portrayal of black men in film. To Lee, this was the opportunity to take back the image of the black man that to date, in Lee's view, had been completely constructed by the white man. It was the opportunity to not only recolor the black man, it was Lee's chance to make it in film.

> Vowing to cut no corners, Lee planned a biographical film of epic proportions that required months of research, numerous interviews, and even an unprecedented trip to Saudi Arabia for authentic-looking footage of Malcolm's pilgrimage to the holy

---

[223] Herman Gray, "Black Masculinity and Visual Culture," *Callaloo* 18.2 (1995).

[224] Phillip Brian Harper, "Walk-on Parts and Speaking Subjects; Screen Representations of Black Gay Men," *Callaloo,* 18.2 (1995).

city of Mecca. Taken shortly before his assassination in 1965, this journey caused a significant change in Malcolm's political and religious outlook. The final product traces Malcolm X's development from his impoverished, rural roots to his final years as an electrifying speaker and leader. 'I knew this was going to be the toughest thing I ever did,' Lee told *Time*. 'The film is huge in the canvas we had to cover and in the complexity of Malcolm X.'[225]

Lee fought tooth and nail to win the right to direct the film and to defend his vision of Malcolm X from the start. When he learned of plans by Warner Bros. to make *Malcolm X*, Norman Jewison had already been chosen as its director. After Lee told the *New York Times* that he had a 'big problem' with a white man directing the film, Jewison agreed to bow out. Not all reactions to Lee's production were positive.[226]

According to Bell Hooks:

Despite continuing hype that depicts him as an outsider struggling against the white movie-industry establishment, Lee is by now an insider, able, say, to force Warner to hire him as director of Malcolm X instead of the white filmmaker initially chosen. The folks at Warner were likely unmoved by Spike's narrow identity politics—his insistence that for a white man to make the film would be 'wrong with a capital W.' Rather, they recognized that his presence would draw the bigger crossover audience, and thus ensure the movie's financial success.[227]

Moreover, according to Hooks,

[i]t is equally true that there is no place for black militant rage in Hollywood. Finally, it is Malcolm's militancy that the film erases. Lee seems primarily fascinated not by Malcolm the political revolutionary—not by the critique of racism in conjunction with imperialism and colonialism, and certainly not by the

---

[225] J. C. Simpson, "Words with Spike Lee," Time (23 Nov. 1992).

[226] Simpson

[227] Bell Hooks, "Consumed by Images: Analysis of the Movie Malcolm X," *Culture Wars Art Forum* (Feb 1993): 2.

critique of capitalism—but by Malcolm's early view of racism as a masculinity phalocentric power-struggle between black men and white men. Thus the film's major moment of political resistance is the episode in which Malcolm galvanizes Nation of Islam men in a face-off with white men around the issue of police brutality, scenes in which he is portrayed as a Hitler-type leader, ruling with an iron clad fist. Deflecting attention away from the righteous resistance that catalyzed the confrontation, the film makes it appear that all this is a 'dick thing'; yet another shoot out at the OK corral. But that, too, is Hollywood at its best, for this is one of the movie's more powerful sections.[228]

So, for all the hype and for Lee's "authentic blackness," he did not get it right either.

---

[228] Hooks 2.

CHAPTER SIXTEEN
ENVISIONING THE REPRESENTATIONAL BLACK MAN

The controlling images of black men have gone through a metamorphosis. The metamorphosis is however, incomplete. The most vexing problem with the representation of black men on the silver screen is that it is not only moribund, but continues to be penis-centric. James Baldwin put it best:

> I think that I know something about the American masculinity which most of the men in my generation do not know because they have not been menaced by it in a way that I have been. It is still true, alas, that to be an American Negro male is also to be kind of a walking phallic symbol; which means that one pays, in one's personality, for the sexual insecurity of others.[229]

Beliefs that reduce black men to their penises, especially penises that are not under the control of white men, have been largely responsible for constructing the representation of the black buck rapist of Jim Crow time. These beliefs also resulted in an increasingly flat, binary, and hollow representation of black men. This theme has been reintroduced into modern representation of black men even by some black filmmakers, actors, writers, and producers. Movies such as *Colors*, *Boyz in the Hood,* and *Menace II Society* were supposed to present an oppositional view to black men construction. Instead, they ended up

---

[229] James Baldwin, *Nobody Knows My Name* (New York: Vintage, 1963) 178.

presenting the same penis-centric portrayal, except this time in black face.

The black men in these films simply constructed "black masculinity," not counter hegemonic portrayals. Constructing black masculinity is not in and of itself a problem. However, the black masculinity created by these films is steeped in black heterosexual prowess. Like other binaries of the black male portrayal, women are required in order to actualize this type of masculinity. In order for this construction to work, the black male must have multiple female sexual partners, must dominate women in their relationships, or father children out of wedlock in order to prove virility. The fact that a film is "black" does not make the construction any more acceptable than buck, Coon, Tom, or Nigger.

Black men are not a homogenous group and should not be constructed and represented as such on film. All black men are not defined and confined by the size of their penises and should not be portrayed as such. Black men have made significant contributions to American intellectual, political, and cultural milieu, but such contributions have rarely found their way into film. Films such as Michael Romer's *Nothing but a Man* (1964), Charles Burnett's *Killer of Sheep* (1977), and Billy Woodberry's *Bless Their Little Hearts* (1984) at least begin to lay bare the complexity of the black man and represent the complexity in film.

These films are not simply representations of a commoditized, pseudo-gangsta thug imagery that in modern times is the new *Birth of a Nation* in Timberlands. All of these productions attempt to place the black protagonist in an institutional context. Placing a black man in an institutional context in film brings to the fore the fact that the complexity of the black man is not simply rooted in his never-ending erection, his fragile masculinity, his bed and breed proclivities, nor his addiction to drugs and hyper-masculinity.

This is not to suggest that this is not a reality for some black men, because for some it is. It is to suggest that black men are attracted to and marry black women and white women, they are educated and uneducated, they are bisexual and heterosexual, and they are middle class, rich, and poor. Black men are gay and flamboyant, as well as gay and modest. Black men are athletes, doctors, lawyers, educators, criminals, and just plain lazy. Black men are in committed heterosexual and homosexual relationships; they are single fathers, welfare cheats, drug dealers, drug addicts, HIV negative, and HIV positive.

The problem is that these various representations of black men do not find themselves in films because liberal white filmmakers often fear being called racists if they produce such representations. Black filmmakers, directors, actors, and social justice advocates have become so locked into the positive and negative binaries that for them black men must be represented as either positive or negative, there is no alternative.

Both white liberals and black social justice advocates of the ilk I just described suffer from a myopic, protectionist view of the black male image that is unrealistic and unhelpful. Portraying black men as they are in film does not simply require a paradigm shift, it requires the construction of a new paradigm that is steeped not in how black men should be represented, but in how black men are.

White liberal filmmakers and those black folks who believe they are the keepers of the black male image miss the point. The problem for the black protectionists is that they do not want white folks to know the complexity of the black man, because this will lead to a negative construction of black men. The problem with this "logic" is that white America already knows that the black man is complex. What they do not understand is that the complexity is not based in some rugged individual or latent black gene that passes down what some may call deviant behavior from generation to generation. It is instead based in America's refusal to avoid any serious discussion about the legacy of slavery and discrimination that have become so institutionalized that discrimination, exclusion, and marginalization is as American as motherhood and apple pie. It is therefore easier for Hollywood to present these positive and negative portrayals of black men, realizing that one side will love it and the other side will hate it. The love-hate dichotomy accomplishes exactly what an oppressive culture expects. It produces disagreement about how the oppressed should be constructed and represented. As long as there is disagreement and a positive-negative binary, nothing has to change.

A move to a real construction and representation will not only require Hollywood and white filmmakers, it will require black men to uncouple ideas of male strength and virility from the current system of sexual dominance. It will require that black protectionists resist the temptation to protect the black male image as if they were given the equivalent of a sharecroppers wages in such protection. It will also require the accomplishment of a far more difficult task: that of convincing black and white audiences to support these movies at the box office when they have become so used to the positive-negative, one dimensional binary.[230]

Films such as Michael Romer's, *Nothing but a Man* (1964) Charles Burnett's *Killer of Sheep* (1977), and Billy Woodberry's *Bless Their Little Hearts* (1984) are by no means perfect, nor should we expect them to be. They do, however, do what filmic representations of black men have yet to do. They are aimed at seriously challenging the waif, skinny, malnourished portrayals of black men and offering alternative, not positive portrayals. They make clear that the cinematic black male persona is not simply one dimensional, one track, or "one penis." These movies make clear that the black male representation in film does not serve a single or unifying purpose. That is, he is intended to confront, challenge, entertain, laugh, joke, cry, die, reproduce, and do everything else that black men do off screen. An alternative portrayal will uncouple subordination, heterosexism, penis-centrality, and binary construction.

---

[230] I realize that persons of all backgrounds consume movies. The use of black and white in this context is offered because of the black and white construction in the American historical context.

AFTERWORD

I have written this collection of essays with the hope of beginning a discussion. I will be criticized by some, marginalized by others, praised by yet others, ignored, and vilified. For this, I am grateful, because the conversation about race in America lacks coherence, historical context, and substance. I hope that this edition provides the opportunity for people to examine my essays critically and to reach whatever conclusions they wish to reach. Regardless of whether we choose to admit it, America has not dealt with the issues of race and racism and they are as American as baseball and apple pie. Whites and some blacks want to live in a post-racial society. But how can that happen when America does not even want to admit that racism continues to exist? How can we transcend race when the conversation about race is not about race but about ideology? Why is it that so many Americans want to live in a "color-blind" society when color is a fact of life? The issue is not whether race exists. The issue is whether it matters, and the fact is that it does.

The history of the impact of race on the 2008 U.S. Presidential election has yet to be written and will be covered more fully in the second edition of this book. However, several racial themes have emerged in the primaries and are worthy of discussion here. First, both Barack Obama and Hillary Clinton were race-baited. He initially wanted to be seen as just a candidate and not a black candidate. The media was all too willing to oblige. David Greenberg, assistant professor of journalism and media studies at Rutgers University in New Jersey, said in a

January 13, Washington Post article that Obama's "allure" stems from his "near-perfect pitch in talking about race to white America."[231]

Greenberg quoted social commentators saying that a president Obama would be a "ringing symbol" that racism no longer rules in the United States. That, said Greenberg, makes Obama the "great white hope." Greenberg said many voters and political pundits "remain in-toxicated [...] with the hope" that Obama can "deliver [...] a categori-cally different kind of change" from Hillary Clinton or the Republican presidential candidates. Christopher Hitchens of Slate.com writes,

> One can't exactly say that Sen. Obama himself panders to questions of skin color. One of the best chapters of his charm-ing autobiography describes the moment when his black Re-publican opponent in the Illinois Senate race—Alan Keyes—accused him of possessing insufficient negritude because he wasn't the descendant of slaves! Obama's decision to be light-hearted—and perhaps light-skinned—about this was a mile-stone in itself. But are we not in danger of emulating Keyes' insane mistake every time we bang on about the senator's pig-mentation? If you wanted a 'black' president or vice president so much, you could long ago have turned out en masse for An-gela Davis—also the first woman to be on a national ticket—or for Jesse Jackson or Al Sharpton. So, why didn't you? Could it have been the politics?[232]

The racial subtext here is clear. Obama is not the first black candi-date to run for president, he is the first one that a majority of white people find acceptable. Unlike Davis, he does not have an afro and will not "fight the power;" unlike Jackson, he does not talk in rhymes, and unlike Sharpton he does not advocate for Tawan Brawley. Obama has had to admit that for all his talk of a post-racial America, this is still a racialized America and when the going got tough, he had to talk about race.

---

[231] Christopher Hitchens, "Identity Crisis: There's Something Pathetic and Embarrassing about Our Obsession with Barack Obama's Race," 7 Jan. 2008, *Slate*, 10 May 2008 <http://www.slate.com/id/2181460/>

[232] Hitchens

Clinton initially tried to pretend that she was not running against a black candidate, but simply a candidate. When the going got tough, she played the race card and many Americans, particularly black Americans, were "shocked" that the Clintons would play the race card. The shock, it seems to me, is based on the notion held by many blacks that the Clintons were somehow immune from race-baiting. Why would they be? They have white privilege and are not afraid to use it. Hillary Clinton has often compared herself to Eleanor Roosevelt. "So occasionally, I'll be sitting somewhere and I'll be listening to someone perhaps not saying the kindest things about me. And I'll look down at my hand and I'll sort of pinch my skin to make sure it still has the requisite thickness I know Eleanor Roosevelt expects me to have."[233] Like Roosevelt, Clinton has very defined views on race that evolved over time. Like Roosevelt, she has spoken about formal equality; and like Roosevelt she benefits from white privilege. Like all of us, she lives in a racialized society and so the decisions she makes will be based on the currency of race.

Second, the majority of white journalists, commentators, advocacy journalists, and members of the self-appointed and self-aggrandizing punditry were so afraid to talk about race that they too pretended that Obama was not a black man, but simply a man. He was, they said, the candidate who would "transcend race." Of course, this all changed when Black Liberation Theology was introduced in the person of Obama's pastor, Jeremiah Wright. "The issue of race has been present throughout the contest for the Democratic nomination, and it's bubbling to the surface as the comments of Barack Obama's pastor, the Rev. Jeremiah Wright, have come under scrutiny."[234] "An ABC News review of dozens of Rev. Wright's sermons, offered for sale by the church, found repeated denunciations of the U.S. based on what he de-

---

[233] Hillary Clinton, "I Get Inspiration from Eleanor Roosevelt," *Daily News Staff* (15 Oct. 2007)

[234] Steve Inskeep and David Greene, "Obama Speaks in Philadelphia as Race Debate Flares," *Morning Edition,* 18 Mar. 2008, National Public Radio Online, 10 May 2008 <http://www.npr.org/templates/story/story.php?storyId=88460822>

scribed as his reading of the Gospels and the treatment of black Americans."[235]

> So if the savvy Obama campaign knew Wright was a problem a year ago, why did the Illinois senator, a parish member for two decades, wait until last week to disassociate and denounce the minister's inflammatory statements? [...]The topic is clearly uncomfortable for Obama and his aides, personally and politically. Axelrod's comments came only after prodding from a reporter and after he had initially suggested that Wright's absence that day was due merely to the fact that the temperature was in the single digits.[236]

And so it was that the media found its racial voice. The candidate that was post-racial had now become pre-racial, currently racial, polar-racial, and racialized. It seemed as if Barack had gotten his black back. Many whites who had thought that Obama was not Jesse Jackson or Al Sharpton have become increasingly anxious. Sharpton and Jackson represent the boggie man to many whites; Obama was the post-boggie man, or so they thought. How could he sit in the pews and hear such hate preached against white people they mused, when he himself is half white? Why didn't he just leave the church? Ah, the benefits of white privilege. The fact is that in many black churches on Sunday mornings discussions about race, whites, and oppression are the norm. Of course, since many whites are in white churches on Sunday mornings, they have not heard these sermons. Not wanting to admit that whites are uncomfortable with Wright's blackness, and by extension, Obama's, some have gone straight to the default position, saying that preachers should not use the pulpit to talk politics. "While Wright may have run afoul of IRS regulations, he ultimately violated something much more sacred. In the traditions of both Judaism and Christianity, prophets

---

[235] Brian Ross and Rehabel-Buri, "Obama's Pastor: God Damn America, U.S. to Blame for 9/11. Obama's Pastor, Rev. Jeremiah Wright, Has a History of What Even Obama's Campaign Aides Say Is 'Inflammatory Rhetoric,'" 13 Mar. 2008, *ABC News Online*, 10 May 2008 <http://abc news.go.com/Blotter/story?id=4443788&page=1>

[236] Peter Wallsten, "Top of the Ticket," 16 Mar. 2008, *Politics Coast to Coast with the LA Times*, blog, 10 May 2008 <http://latimesblogs. latimes.com/washington/2008/03/throughout-his.html> par. 8.

spoke God's truth to the people, calling their audience to repentance for its own actions."[237] "The Rev. Jeremiah Wright, Jr. preaches that he follows the righteous path, but when it comes to the federal tax law, his Trinity United Church of Christ may have crossed the line."[238]

They have conveniently forgotten about the four platforms of the Moral Majority:

- **Platform #1**: The Moral Majority Coalition will conduct an intensive "Voter Registration Campaign" through America's conservative churches, para-church ministries, pro-life and pro-family organizations.
- **Platform #2**: The Moral Majority Coalition will conduct well organized "Get-Out-The-Vote Campaigns" in 2008.
- **Platform #3**: The Moral Majority Coalition will engage in the massive recruitment and mobilization of social conservatives through television, radio, direct mail (U.S.P.S. and Internet) and public rallies.
- **Platform #4**: The Moral Majority Coalition will encourage the promotion of continuous private and corporate prayer for America's moral renaissance based on 2 Chronicles 7:14.[239]

They must have also forgotten that Dr. Dobson of Focus on the Family is openly political.

In a letter his aides say is being sent to more than one million of his supporters, Dr. Dobson, the child psychologist and founder of the evangelical organization Focus on the Family, promises 'a battle of enormous proportions from sea to shining

[237] Greg Johnson, "Politics in the Pulpit," 30 Mar. 2008, *knoxnews.com*, 10 May 2008 <http://www.knoxnews.com/news/2008/mar/30/johnson-politics-pulpit/> par. 14.

[238] Jeff Goldblat, "Obama's Spiritual Mentor May Put Church in Hot Water," 12 Mar. 2008, *FoxNews.com*, 10 May 2008 <http://elections.foxnews.com/2008/03/12/obamas-controversial-pastor-puts-church-in-hot-water/> par. 2.

[239] The Moral Majority Coalition, 10 May 2008 <http://www. moral-majority.com/>.

sea' if President Bush fails to appoint 'strict constructionist' jurists or if Democrats filibuster to block conservative nominees.

Dr. Dobson recalled the conservative efforts that helped in the November defeat of Senator Tom Daschle of South Dakota, the Senate minority leader who led Democrats in using the filibuster to block 10 of Mr. Bush's judicial nominees.

'Let his colleagues beware,' Dr. Dobson warned, 'especially those representing 'red' states. Many of them will be in the 'bull's-eye' the next time they seek re-election.'

He singled out Ben Nelson of Nebraska, Mark Dayton of Minnesota, Robert C. Byrd of West Virginia, Kent Conrad of North Dakota, Jeff Bingaman of New Mexico and Bill Nelson of Florida. All six are up for re-election in 2006.[240]

In true post-racial America parlance, the lines are blurred. The issue is not using the pulpit to talk about politics, it is black liberation theology. Many whites have become afraid, very afraid. Who, they ask themselves is Obama? Is he an undercover radical? Sensing a looming political crisis, Obama's campaign delivered a major address on race in Philadelphia where Obama would get his black back. Among the highlights, Wright's statements were controversial and divisive and racially charged. He said, "The white community must start acknowledging that what ails the African-American community does not exist in the minds of black people: that the legacy of discrimination and current incidents of discrimination, while less overt than in the past are real and must be addressed."[241] But, what does this mean? What does he plan to do to address it? Will electing him president pay America's debt for its legacy of discrimination? Will his election be so historic that whites can say that race no longer matters in America? Can he be a black president? What is a black president anyway? If he is elected and is not a black president, then how will blacks react to that? Will they level the

---

[240] David D. Kirkspatrick, "Evangelical Leader Threatens to Use His Political Muscle Against Some Democrats," *The New York Times,* 1 Jan. 2005.

[241] *The New York Times*, "Barack Obama's Speech on Race," 18 Mar. 2008, *Politics*, 10 May 2008 <http://www.nytimes.com/2008/03/ 18/us/ politics/18text-obama.html?pagewanted=5acessced>

same charges that they have against whites that he does not understand their issues or that he took their votes for granted? Should he be elected President, will this give white Americans the opportunity that so many of them have been waiting for to say, "We don't want to hear about racism, about civil rights, about justice, about racial profiling anymore. You have your black President...now get over it!" What will change in the lives of the average black person in America should he be elected? Would the symbolism of his election be enough? Enough for whom? For how long?

Some praised the speech, others ignored it, and the media overanalyzed it. However, after the speech, Obama once again caused some whites to ask whether he had gotten too much black back when speaking on a Philadelphia sports show he said: "The point I was making was not that Grandmother harbors any racial animosity. She doesn't. But she is a typical white person, who, if she sees somebody on the street that she doesn't know, you know, there's a reaction that's been bred in our experiences that don't go away and that sometimes come out in the wrong way, and that's just the nature of race in our society."[242]

So, who is a typical white person? Larry King, The Huffington Post, Jonah Goldberg of The Nation, and others wondered? "Seriously, Barack Obama basically called all white people racist. [...] Is this guy kidding?" wrote Taylor Marsh of the Huffington Post.[243] Here again, whites who were so comfortable pretending that Obama is not black have had to address the fact that he is. In a post-racial America, this is a source of discomfort for the colorblind advocates. They didn't have to look far or wait long for their answer. Pat Buchanan spoke for typical white people with crystal clarity:

> First, America has been the best country on earth for black folks. It was here that 600,000 black people, brought from Africa in slave ships, grew into a community of 40 million, were

---

[242] Barack Obama, interview, *610 WIP,* host Angelo Cataldi, 20 Mar. 2008.

[243] Taylor Marsh, "Obama: Grandmother Typical White Person." 20 Mar. 2008, *Huffington Post,* 10 May 2008 <http://www.huffingtonpost.com/taylor-marsh/obama-grandmother-typic_b_92601.html>.

introduced to Christian salvation, and reached the greatest levels of freedom and prosperity blacks have ever known. [...]

Second, no people anywhere has done more to lift up blacks than white Americans. Untold trillions have been spent since the '60s on welfare, food stamps, rent supplements, Section 8 housing, Pell grants, student loans, legal services, Medicaid, Earned Income Tax Credits and poverty programs designed to bring the African-American community into the mainstream. Governments, businesses and colleges have engaged in discrimination against white folks—with affirmative action, contract set-asides and quotas—to advance black applicants over white applicants.

Churches, foundations, civic groups, schools and individuals all over America have donated time and money to support soup kitchens, adult education, day care, retirement and nursing homes for blacks.

We hear the grievances. Where is the gratitude?[244]

Regardless of whether one agrees with Buchanan's conservative credentials or his ideology, he says those things that white people in a post-racial America say only in private and shy away from in public. His views are often those views that are expressed by whites when they talk about race with each other. The typical white person in a post-racial America situates racism in the past; embraces formal equality; believes that America has done so much for blacks and yet blacks never seem to think that it is enough; walks on egg shells around blacks for fear that they will say something offensive; believes in inter-racial dating, so long as it is not their son or daughter who is marrying black; does not see themself as racialized, but basks in white privilege; believes that blacks use race as an excuse for failure, that blacks who are successful are the exception; believes that pretending that race doesn't matter makes it true; and still harbors and makes decisions based on preexisting stereotypes.

In a spate of interviews after the speech, he was asked by Anderson Cooper of CNN, whether blacks saw patriotism differently than whites;

---

[244] Patrick Buchanan, "PJB: A Brief for Whitey," 21 Mar. 2008, *Patrick J. Buchanan: Right from the Beginning*, 10 May 2008 <http://www.buchanan.org/blog/?p=969> pars. 17, 19–22.

the subtext being that whites have set the standard for patriotism and that blacks either did not accept it or that black patriotism is somehow linked to our race. That the question was asked by Cooper, not a flame-throwing right-winger, suggests the script for the fall election should Obama be the nominee. For many whites, including liberal and moderate whites, Wright presents the opportunity to exert their racist fears by hiding behind patriotism or the lack thereof. The strategy will be to paint Obama as unpatriotic because of his association with Wright. Whites can feel comfortable saying that they are not against Obama because of his race, but because he is unpatriotic. As "evidence" they will use the words of Wright, Obama's failure to wear the American flag pin on his lapel, and the comment made by his wife that this is the first time in a long time that she is proud to be an American.

A post-racial America provides whites with the opportunity to declare that race does not matter, but that in any event one cannot elect a president who is unpatriotic. This is a powerful, though intellectually bankrupt argument given the premise, which is that whites define patriotism and that should blacks veer from that definition, then they are unpatriotic. One wonders how a patriotic country allows many of its citizens to be routinely disenfranchised. How patriotic it is to run political ads that promote racial division as a ploy to win elections? To be sure, patriotism is critical to the survival of America and the core values of American democracy. But, doesn't patriotism also have ethical dimensions? Where is the moral standard or moral value when some would choose to question a candidate's patriotism, based not on evidence, but on conjecture rife with racial animus? The fact is that any attempt to question another's patriotism is a serious matter and we will see that in a post-racial America many will blur the lines between defining patriotism on the one hand and scandalous race-baiting on the other. The question is, can America see the difference.

Obama's success in post-racial politics has ramifications for other black politicians also dubbed post-racial by the press. Consider the case of black Philadelphia Mayor Michael A. Nutter. Nutter endorsed Hillary Clinton, and unlike some other black politicians, such as Congressman John Lewis of Georgia, did not switch his support to Obama because it was politically expedient to do so. Seeming to take Nutter to task for the fact that he should back Obama because of his race, Paul Vitello writes in the *New York Times*:

> Mr. Obama, the Illinois and presidential candidate, is wildly popular here, especially in the poor black neighborhoods and the upper-income white neighborhoods that gave Mr. Nutter his greatest margins of victory. But Mr. Nutter has endorsed Senator Hillary Rodham Clinton of New York in the pivotal Democratic presidential primary in Pennsylvania on April 22. In some ways, the question that the endorsement has raised is the Rubick's Cube at the core of the 'post-racial' politics that both he and Mr. Obama represent; if Mr. Obama's candidacy is a historical racial benchmark, how do you introduce that idea into political discourse without reference to the old racial politics that give the benchmark its meaning?[245]

Although the concept of a post-racial America enjoys wide-spread support in the media, this article and the handling of the Obama candidacy so far demonstrate that the gap between rhetoric and reality is wide and getting wider. The challenge is to close the gap. The problem, of course, is that closing the gap requires addressing the lingering effects of racism and discrimination, which begins with an honest conversation of race and racism. This, it seems, is too much to ask for an America fond of shying away from tough issues deeply invested in barren hyperbole.

The full effect of the Wright controversy and what it says about a post-racial America will only be known if Obama is the Democratic nominee and has to face a general election in which the 527s will, in Willie Horton and Harold Ford Junior style, produce ads and vile video that will link Obama, Wright, Jesse Jackson, Al Sharpton, Malcolm X, Louis Farrakhan, and Olympians Tommie Smith and John Carlos, who raised their fists in the black power salute at the 1968 Summer Olympics. The message will be clear: A post-racial America has its limits. John McCain will distance himself from the issue; the ads will eventually be pulled after they have been played incessantly on television and the Internet. Many will take to the lecterns and state that we have no

---

[245] Paul Vitelo, "A Mayor in the Obama Mold, but Backing Clinton," *The New York Times,* 14 Apr. 2008.

place for this kind of racial politics in America and the damage will be done.

How can Obama transcend race when race is so central to American life? Obama has discussed the lingering effects of race, he has not addressed it. By failing to address race in any substantive way and instead choosing to "discuss" the topic in such vacuous and empty abstractions, the media has, thus far, proven their own level of discomfort with their own inner racial demons. Jeremiah Wright gave them permission to bring to the surface what has always been present.

There has been much discussion in the media as to whether blacks were voting for Obama because he is black and because many blacks thought that their time had come to make history by helping to elect a black president. The subtext is that it would be wrong for blacks to vote for a candidate simply because he is black, since this would be tantamount to Affirmative Action. The fact is that many blacks did vote for Obama because he is black and there is nothing wrong with that, since many whites voted for John Edwards because he is white, for Bill Clinton because he is white, against Jesse Jackson because he is black, and against Tom Bradley who ran for Governor of California because he is black; the list goes on and on.

Given that America is a racialized society, we need to address the question of how a racialized society impacts the decisions that we all make, rather than seeking to castigate people for making racialized decisions. Discussions about racism and its continuing significance in all aspects of American life are akin to the person who has a terminal illness and pretends that if they ignore it, it will go away. This election is widely cast as historic for a number of reasons. However, perhaps it is historic because the Democratic Party has recast itself as caring so much about blacks and is being accused by many blacks of taking their votes for granted when they can nominate a black candidate. The Democratic Party, however, is not the entire American electorate.

Finally, this "historic" election proves that many liberal whites and some conservative whites may be comfortable voting for Obama, because they have constructed him as the "Acceptable" Negro (read Sidney Poitier in Guess Whose Coming to Dinner?) rather than the "Maddening Negro" (read Lucas Beauchamp in Intruder in the Dust).

I have taught students in both undergraduate and graduate courses in civil rights and I have become concerned that there is a generation of students who have convinced themselves that racial discrimination was outlawed some time ago (although many don't know when) and that this ends the matter. First, outlawing racial discrimination does not end the matter; it is a beginning. Second, these students simply do not have enough historical and contextual knowledge to deconstruct the realities of racism to reach a conclusion that is solidified by logic and reality. Third, race-baiting has become an integral part of American politics, policy, and some organizational cultures. Organizations that have chosen to respond to this do so by conducting diversity and sensitivity training in which racism is rarely discussed in any substantive way.

Finally, this edition of essays is dedicated to students everywhere whom I believe must take responsibility for their own learning and make their own decisions on race and racism. In so doing, I hope there will be both conversation and action, and that reasoned discussion will replace naked vitriol and empty rhetoric and inaction. I also hope that when my book *Jim Crow on Steroids: How Soon We Forget, Collusive People of Color, and the New and More Potent Form of Racism* (now in production) is available, that people will be ready to read it.

BIBLIOGRAPHY

50 Cent Feat Hot Rod, "I Got Hoes." *DJ White Owl & 50 Cent-Fully Loaded-Mixfiend.* 2007.

African American Odyssey: A Quest for Full Citizenship. 21 Mar. 2008. The Library of Congress On-line Exhibition. 10 May 2008 <lcweb2 .loc.gov/ammem/aaohtml/exhibit/aopart7.html>.

Allen, Theodore W. *The Invention of the White Race,* I. London: Verso. 1994.

Anderson, Carol. *Eyes off the Prize: The United Nations and the African American Struggle for Human Rights, 1944–1955.* Cambridge, UK: Cambridge University Press, 2003.

Anderson, Carol. "Human Rights at Home." Keynote address. Women's Foundation of California, San Francisco, California, 11 Jan. 2006.

Baldwin, James. *Nobody Knows My Name.* New York: Vintage, 1963.

Baltzell, E. Digby. Introduction, *A Social Study,* by W. E. B. Du Bois. New York: Shocken Books, 1967.

Beal, Frances M. "Warped Lens Distorts Mississippi Burning." 27 Feb. 1989. *Frontline.* 10 May 2008 <http://www.hartford-hwp.com /archives /45a/453.html> .

Beck, Francis J. *Affirmative Action: Social Justice or Reverse Discrimination?* Amherst, NY: Prometheus Books, 1997.

Bell, Derrick A., Jr. "Brown v. Board of Education and the Interest-Convergence Dilemma." *Harvard Law Rev.* 93.3 (Jan. 1980): 518–533.

Bell, Derrick. "Racial Realism," *Connecticut Law Review* 24.2 (1992): 363–379.

Berg, Manfred. "Black Civil Rights and Liberal Anticommunism: The NAACP in the Early Cold War." *The Journal of American History* 94.1 (2007): 49 pars. 14 Mar. 2008 <http://www.historycooperative.org /journals/jah/94.1/berg.html>.

Berkhoffer, Robert E. *The White Man's Indian*. New York: Vintage, 1978.

"Blacks in American Film," *AfricanAmericans.com*. 10 May 2008 <http://www.africanamericans.com/Films.htm>.

Blauner, Robert. *Racial Oppression in America*. New York: Harper and Row, 1972.

Boas, Franz. *Anthropology and Modern Life*. New York: W.W. Norton, 1962.

Bogle, Donald. *Toms, Coons, Mulattoes, Mammies, and Bucks*. New York: Viking Press, 1973.

Brenkman, J. *Culture and Domination*. Ithaca: Cornell Univ. Press, 1987.

Brooks, Thomas R. *Walls Come Tumbling Down: A History of the Civil Rights Movement: 1940–1970*. Englewood Cliffs, NJ: Prentice-Hall 1974.

Brownlow, K. *Behind the Mask of Innocence*. Berkley: University of California, 1990.

Buchanan, Allen E. *Secession: The Morality of Political Divorce from Fort Sumter to Lithuania and Quebec*. Boulder Colorado: Westview Press, 1990.

Buchanan, Allen E. "The Right to Self-Determination: Analytical and Moral Foundations." *Ariz. J. Int'l & Comp. L.* 8 (1991): 41, 48.

Buchanan, Allen E. "Federalism, Secession, and the Morality of Inclusion." *Ariz. L. Rev.* 37 (1995): 53, 54.

Buchanan, Patrick. "PJB: A Brief for Whitey." 21 Mar. 2008. *Patrick J. Buchanan: Right from the Beginning*. 10 May 2008 <http://www.buchanan.org/blog/?p=969>.

Cassese, Antonio. *International Law*. New York: Oxford University Press, 2005.

Charen, Mona. *Do-Gooders: How Liberals Hurt Those They Claim to Help (and the Rest of Us)*. New York, New York: Penguin Group, Dec. 2004.

Civil Rights Act of 1875, 18 Stat. 335 (1875).

Civil Rights Cases, 109 U.S. 3 (1883) (109).

Clinton, Hillary. "I Get Inspiration from Eleanor Roosevelt." *Daily News Staff.* 15 Oct. 2007.

Collins, Patricia Hill. *Black Sexual Politics.* New York: Routledge, 2005.

Connell, Robert. "Masculinities and Globalization," *Men's Lives.* Eds. M. S. Kimmel and M. A. Messner. Meedham Heights: Allyn and Bacon, 2000.

Crenshaw, K. W. "Race Reform, Retrenchment: Transformation and Legitimization in Anti-Discrimination Law." *Harvard L. Rev.*, 101 (1988): 1331–1387.

Crenshaw, Kimberle. "Mapping the Margins: Intersectionality, Identity Politics, and Violence against Women of Color." *Stanford Law Review* 43.6 (Jul. 1991): 1241–1299.

Crenshaw, Kimberle, and Gary Peller. "The Contradictions of Mainstream Constitutional Theory." *UCLA L. Rev.* 45 (1998): 1683–1716.

Cross, Theodore L. *The Black Power Imperative: Racial Inequality and the Politics of Nonviolence.* New York: Faulkner, 1987.

Davis, Ronald L. F. "Creating Jim Crow: In-Depth Essay." *The History of Jim Crow.* New York Life. 10 May 2008 <http://www.jimcrow history.org/history/creating2.htm>.

D'Emilio, J., and E.B. Freedman. *Intimate Matters: A History of Sexuality in America.* New York: Harper and Row, 1988.

Diawara, Manthia. *The Blackface Stereotype.* 1998. 10 May 2008 <www.blackculturalstudies.org> .

Dolan, C. "Collapsing Masculinities and Weak States: A Case Study From Northern Uganda." *Masculinities Matter! Men, Gender and Development.* Ed. F. Cleaver. London & New York: Zed Books, 2002.

Dominguez, Virginia. *White by Definition: Social Classification in Creole Louisiana.* New Brunswick: Rutgers University Press, 1986.

Dred Scott v. Sandford, 60 U.S. 393, 1857.

D'Souza, D. *The End of Racism: Principles for a Multiracial Society.* New York: Free Press, 1995.

Du Bois, W. E. B. *The Suppression of the African Slave Trade to the United States of America, 1638–1870.* Diss., Harvard. New York: Longmans, 1904.

Du Bois, W. E. B. "Opinion." *The Crisis,* Nov. 1910.

Du Bois, W. E. B. "Opinion." *The Crisis,* Nov. 1913.

Du Bois, W. E. B. Editorial. *The Crisis,* May 1924.

Du Bois, W. E. B. *Dusk of Dawn: An Essay Toward an Autobiography of a Race Concept,* 1940. New York: Schocken Books, 1968.

Du Bois, W. E. B. Memo to Walter White. 23 Aug. 1948.

Dudziak, Mary L. *Cold War Civil Rights: Race and the Image of American Democracy.* Princeton U, 2000.

Duncan, Otis A. "Patterns of Occupational Mobility Among Negro Men." *Demography* 5.1 (1968): 11–22.

Dyer, Richard. "White." *Screen* 29.4 (1988): 44–64.

Emerson, Jim. *Mississippi Burning.* 1988. 10 May 2008 <http://cinepad.com/reviews/mississippi.htm>.

Farley, Anthony Paul. "The Black Body as Fresh Object." *Oregon Law Review* 76 (1997): 457–535.

"Final Warning: A History of the New World Order." *The Modern History Project.* 10 Mar. 2008 <http://www.modernhistoryproject.org/mhp/ArticleDisplay.php?Article=FinalWarn04>.

Finkleman, Paul. "The Crime of Color." *Tul. L. Rev.* 67 (1993): 2063, 2081-87.

Foreman, Murray, and Mark Anthony Neal, eds. *That's the Joint! The Hip-Hop Studies Reader.* New York: Rutledge, 2004.

Frankenberg, R. *White Women, Race Matters: The Social Construction of Whiteness.* Minneapolis: University of Minnesota Press, 1993.

Freeman, Michael. *Human Rights: An Interdisciplinary Approach.* Hoboken, New Jersey: Wiley & Sons, Inc., 2002.

Garvey, Marcus. Editorial. *The Negro World,* 13 Feb. 1923.

Gavin, Michael. "Intertemporal Dimensions of International Economic Adjustment: Evidence from the Franco-Prussian War Indemnity." *The American Economic Review,* 82.2, Papers and Proceedings of the Hundred and Fourth Annual Meeting of the American Economic Association (May 1992): 174–179.

Genovese, Eugene. *Red and Black: Marxian Explorations in Southern and Afroamerican History.* New York: Pantheon, 1980.

George Washington University. "Eleanor Roosevelt and Civil Rights." *The Eleanor Roosevelt Papers Project.* 10 Mar. 2008 <http://www.gwu.edu/~erpapers/teachinger/lesson-plans/notes-er-and-civil-rights.cfm>.

George Washington University. "Teaching Eleanor Roosevelt Glossary: Walter White (1893–1955)." The Eleanor Roosevelt Papers Project. 10 Mar. 2008 <http://www.gwu.edu/~erpapers/teachinger/glossary/white-walter.cfm>.

Georgia Humanities Council and the University of Georgia Press. "Walter White." 2008. *The New Georgia Encyclopedia.* 10 May 2008 <http://www.georgiaencyclopedia.org/nge/Article.jsp?id=h-747>.

Goldblat, Jeff. "Obama's Spiritual Mentor May Put Church in Hot Water." 12 Mar. 2008. *FoxNews.com.* 10 May 2008 <http://elections.foxnews.com/2008/03/12/obamas-controversial-pastor-puts-church-in-hot-water/>.

Gossett, Thomas. *Race: The History of An Idea in America.* Dallas: Southern Methodist University Press, 1963.

Gray, Herman. "Black Masculinity and Visual Culture." *Callaloo* 18.2 (1995): 401–405.

Guerrero, Ed. *Framing Blackness*: *The African American Image in Film.* Philadelphia: Temple University Press, 1993.

Guerrero, Ed. "The Black Man on Our Screens and the Empty Space in Representation." *Callaloo* 18.2 (Spring 1995): 395–400.

Hacker, Andrew. *Two Nations Black and White, Separate, Hostile, Unequal.* New York: Scribner's, 1992.

Harper, Phillip Brian. "Walk-on Parts and Speaking Subjects; Screen Representations of Black Gay Men." *Callaloo,* 18.2 (1995): 390–394.

Harris, Robert L., Jr. "Coming of Age: The Transformation of Afro-American Historiography." *Journal of Negro History* 67.2 (1982): 107–121.

Henderson, Errol A. "Black Nationalism and Rap Music." *Journal of Black Studies,* Jan. 1996. 10 May 2008 <www.nbufront.org/html /fvwin98/erroll.html>.

Hernandez-Truyol, Esperanza Berta. "Breaking Cycles of Inequality: Critical Theory, Human Rights, and Family Injustice." *Crossroads, Directions, and a New Critical Race Theory.* Eds. Francisco Valdes, Jerome McCristal Culp, and Angela P. Harris. Philadelphia: Temple University Press, 2002.

Hitchens, Christopher. "Identity Crisis: There's Something Pathetic and Embarrassing about Our Obsession with Barack Obama's Race." 7 Jan. 2008. *Slate.* 10 May 2008 <http://www.slate.com/ id/2181460/>.

Hooks, Bell. "Consumed by Images: Analysis of the Movie Malcolm X." *Culture Wars Art Forum* (Feb 1993).

Hynes, Gerald C. *Biographical Sketch of W. E. B. Du Bois.* 10 May 2008 <http://www.duboislc.org/html/DuBoisBio.html>.

Inskeep, Steve, and David Greene. "Obama Speaks in Philadelphia as Race Debate Flares." *Morning Edition.* 18 Mar. 2008. National Public Radio Online. 10 May 2008 <http://www.npr.org/templates /story/story.php?storyId=88460822>.

Jay-Z. "Ain't No Nigga." *Reasonable Doubt.* 1996.

Jefferson, Thomas. Declaration of Independence of the United States of America. Preamble, 1776.

Johnson, Greg. "Politics in the Pulpit." 30 Mar. 2008. *knoxnews.com.* 10 May 2008 <http://www.knoxnews.com/news/2008/mar/30/ johnson-politics-pulpit/>.

Jordan, Winthrop D. *White Over Black: American Attitudes Toward the Negro, 1550–1812.* Chapel Hill, North Carolina: University of North Carolina Press, 1995.

Jovanovic, M. "Recognizing Minority Identities through Collective Rights." *Human Rights Quarterly* 27 (2005): 625–651.

Junior M.A.F.I.A. "Player's Anthem." *Conspiracy.* Big Beat, 1995.

Kimmel, Michael. Foreward. *Masculinities Matter! Men, Gender and Development.* Ed. F. Cleaver. London & New York: Zed Books, 2002.

Kirkspatrick, David D. "Evangelical Leader Threatens to Use His Political Muscle Against Some Democrats." *The New York Times* 1 Jan. 2005.

Klinkner, Philip A., and Rogers M. Smith. *The Unsteady March.* Chicago: University of Chicago Press, 1999.

Kuklick, Bruce. *American Policy and the Division of Germany: The Clash with Russia over Reparations.* Ithaca, New York: Cornell University Press, 1972.

Leavy, Walter. "50 Years of Black Love in Movies – Special 50th Anniversary Feature." Ebony (Feb 1995). 10 May 2008 <http://findarticles.com/p/articles/mi_m1077/is_n4_v50/ai_16412385>.

Lincoln, Abraham. *The Collected Works of Abraham Lincoln.* Eds. Roy Basler, Marion Dolores Pratt, and Lloyd A. Dunlap. New Brunswick, NJ: Rutgers University Press, 1953–55.

Lipsitz, George. *The Possessive Investment in Whiteness: How White People Profit From Identity Politics.* Philadelphia: Temple UP, 1998.

Logan, Rayford. *The Negro in the United States: A Brief History.* Princeton, New Jersey: Van Nostrand, 1957.

Lopez, Ian F. Haney. *White By Law.* New York University Press, 1996.

Loving v. Virginia, 388 U.S. 1.

Lusk Committee. *Revoluntionary Radicalism.* New York State Legislature, 1920.

Mahmud, Sakah S. "The State and Human Rights in Africa in the 1990s: Perspectives and Prospects." *Hum. Rts. Q.* 15 (1993): 485-98.

Marsh, Taylor. "Obama: Grandmother Typical White Person." 20 Mar. 2008. *Huffington Post.* 10 May 2008 <http://www.huffingtonpost.com/taylor-marsh/obama-grandmother-typic_b_92601.html>.

McIntosh, Peggy. "White Privilege: Unpacking the Invisible Knapsack." *Peace and Freedom* (July/August 1989). Working Paper 189.

Meier, August, and John H. Bracey, Jr. "The NAACP as a Reform Movement, 1909–1965: To Reach the Conscience of America." *The Journal of Southern History* 59.1 (Feb. 1993): 3–30.

Messerschmidt, James W. "We Must Protect Our Southern Women: On Whiteness, Masculinities, and Lynching." *Race, Gender, and Pun-*

ishment: From Colonialism to the War on Terror. Eds. M. Bosworth and J. Flavin. New Brunswick, NJ: Rutgers University Press, 2006) 77–94.

Mills, Charles W. *The Racial Contract.* Ithaca and London: Cornell University Press, 1997.

Mitchell, Clarence. Letter to Louis E. Hosch. 1 Mar. 1950. Box H126, File "Loyalty Review Cases, 1947–1951."

Mkutu, Kennedy. "A Critical Analysis of the Contributions of Notable Black Economists." *Economic Affairs* 25.1 (2005): 63–64.

Moore, Henrietta L. *A Passion for Difference: Essays in Anthropology and Gender.* Cambridge: Polity Press, 1994.

Moral Majority Coalition. 10 May 2008 <http://www.moralmajority.com/>.

Morrison, Rodney J. "Gulf War Reparations: Iraq, OPEC, and the Transfer Problem." *American Journal of Economics and Sociology,* 51.4 (Oct. 1992): 385–399.

Mosher, D. L. and M. Sirkin. "Measuring a Macho Personality Constellation." *Journal of Research and Personality 18* (1984): 150–163.

Moynihan, Patrick. "The Negro Family: The Case for National Action." [Otherwise known as the Moynihan Report.] Washington, D.C.: U.S. Department of Labor, 1965.

Mukerji, Chandra and Michael Schudson, eds. Introduction. *Rethinking Popular Culture: Contemporary Perspectives in Cultural Studies.* Berkley: University of California Press, 1991.

Murray, Hugh T., Jr. "The NAACP versus the Communist Party: The Scottsboro Rape Cases, 1931–1932." *Phylon* 28.3 (3rd Qtr., 1967): 276–287.

NAACP. "Black American History, a History of Black People in the United States." *Africanaonline.* 10 Jan. 2007 <http://www.african aonline.com/orga_naacp.htm>.

Nachbar, Jack, and Kevin Lause. *Popular Culture.* Bowling Green: University Popular Press, 1992.

New York Evening Post. Editorial. 3 Oct. 1897.

New York Times. "Barack Obama's Speech on Race." 18 Mar. 2008. *Politics.* 10 May 2008 <http://www.nytimes.com/2008/03/18/us/politics/18text-obama.html?pagewanted=5acessced>.

Newman, Mark. "Civil Rights and Human Rights." *Reviews in American History* 32.2 (Jun 2004): 247–254.

Nickel, James W. *Making Sense of Human Rights: Philosophical Reflections on the Universal Declaration of Human Rights.* Berkeley: University of California Press, 1987.

Obama, Barack. Interview. *610 WIP,* host Angelo Cataldi, 20 March 2008.

Office of the United Nations High Commissioner for Human Rights (OHCHR). *Leaflet No.2: Indigenous Peoples, the UN and Human Rights.* 10 Jan. 2008 <http://www.ohchr.org/Documents/ Publications/GuideIPleaflet2en.pdf>.

Ottley, Roi. *New World A'Coming: Inside Black America.* Boston: Houghton Mifflin, Life-in-America Books, 1943.

Patterson, William L., ed. *We Charge Genocide.* New York: International Publishers, 1970.

Peck, Mary Gray. Speech. The General Federation of Women's Clubs, 1917.

Perry, Imani. *Prophets of the Hood: Politics and Poetics in Hip Hop.* Duke University Press, 2004.

Peters, J. *The Communist Party: A Manual on Organization.* New York City: Workers Library Publishers, July 1935.

Plessey v. Ferguson, 163 U.S. 537, 1896.

"President's Committee on Civil Rights: Truman's Response to the Cold War Battle in the International Media." 10 Mar. 2008 <http:// www.piedmontcommunities.us/servlet/go_ProcServ/dbpage=page &gid= 0133600115108233325 3641240>.

Ransdall, Hollace. "Report on the Scottsboro, Ala. Case." *Famous American Trials: 'The Scottsboro Boys' Trials 1931–1937.* University of Missouri-Kansas City School of Law. 11 May 2008 <http://www.law.umkc.edu/faculty/projects/FTrials/scottsboro/SB_ HRrep.html#Negroes%20Tried%20in%20Four%20Separate%20C ases>.

Record, Wilson. *Race and Radicalism: The NAACP and the Communist Party in Conflict.* Cornell University Press, 1964.

Rogin, M. "The Sword Became a Flashing Vision." Ed. D. W. Griffith. "The Birth of a Nation," *Representations* 9 (Winter, 1985) 150–195.

Roosevelt, Eleanor. "The Negro and Social Change: A Speech before the National Urban League." *Opportunity* (Jan. 1936): 22–23.

Roosevelt, Eleanor, "Why I Do Not Choose to Run." *Look.* 9 Jul. 1946. Anna Eleanor Roosevelt Papers, Franklin D. Roosevelt Library, Hyde Park, New York.

Roosevelt, Eleanor. "Some of My Best Friends are Negro." Originally printed in *Ebony* 9 (Feb. 1953): 16-20, 22, 24-26, 13 Aug. 2008 <http://newdeal.feri.org/er/er09.htm>.

Ross, Brian, and Rehabel-Buri. "Obama's Pastor: God Damn America, U.S. to Blame for 9/11. Obama's Pastor, Rev. Jeremiah Wright, Has a History of What Even Obama's Campaign Aides Say Is 'Inflammatory Rhetoric.'" 13 Mar. 2008. *ABC News Online.* 10 May 2008 <http://abcnews.go.com/Blotter/story?id=4443788&page=1>.

Ross, Marlon B. *Manning the Race: Reforming Black Men in the Jim Crow Era* (New York: New York UP, 2004) 7.

Ross, Thomas. "The Unbearable Whiteness of Being." *Crossroads, Directions, and a New Critical Race Theory.* Eds. Francisco Valdes, Jerome McCristal Culp, and Angela P. Harris. Philadelphia: Tempe University Press, 2002. 253–254.

Rudwick, Elliott M. "W. E. B. Du Bois in the Role of Crisis Editor." *The Journal of Negro History* 43.3 (Jul. 1958): 214–240.

Russell, Katheryn K. *The Color of Crime: Racial Hoaxes, White Fear, Black Protectionism, Police Harassment, and Other Macroaggressions.* New York: New York University Press, 1997.

Russell, Margaret M. "Race and the Dominant Gaze: Narratives of Law and Inequality in Popular Film." *Legal Studies Forum* 15.3 (1991): 246.

Rutherford, Jonathan. "Who's That Man?" *Male Order: Unwrapping Masculinity.* Eds. R. Chapman and J. Rutherford. London: Lawrence and Wishet, 1988.

Shelton, D. "Righting Wrongs: Reparations in the Articles on State Responsibility." *American Journal of International Law* 96.4 (2002): 833–856.

Sickels, Robert J. *Race, Marriage, and the Law.* Albuquerque: University of New Mexico Press, 1972.

Silva, Fred, ed. *Focus on Birth of a Nation.* Englewood Cliffs, N.J.: Prentice-Hall, 1971.

Simpson, J. C. "Words with Spike Lee." Time, 23 Nov. 1992.

Sklar, R. *Movie Made America.* New York: Random House, 1975.

Slaughter House Cases, 83 U.S. 36, 1873.

Smith, James P., and Finnis R. Welch. *Closing the Gap: Forty Years of Economic Progress for Blacks.* Santa Monica: Rand, 1986.

Snead, J. *White Screen, Black Images: Hollywood from the Dark Side.* New York: Routledge, 1994.

Sowell, Thomas. *Civil Rights: Rhetoric or Reality?* New York: Harper Collins, 1984.

Sowell, Thomas. *Black Rednecks, White Liberals.* San Francisco: Encounter Books, 2005.

Tananbaum, Duane. "The Bricker Amendment Controversy: A Test of Eisenhower's Political Leadership." *Amer. Hist. Rev.* 95.1 (1990): 289.

"The Tom Caricature," *Jim Crow: Museum of Racist Memorabilia.* Ferris State University. 10 May 2008 <http://www.ferris.edu/ jim-crow/tom/>.

Theoharis, Athan G., and John Stuart Cox. T*he Boss: J. Edgar Hoover and the Great American Inquisition* (Philadelphia: Temple UP, 1988).

Truth, Sojourner . "Ain't I A Woman?" Speech. Women's Convention, Akron, Ohio, 1851.

United Nations. "Universal Declaration of Human Rights." Jan. 1997, *Human Rights Web.* 8 Mar. 2008 <www.hrweb.org/legal/udhr. html>.

Valdes, Francisco, Jerome McCristal Culp, and Angela P. Harris, eds. *Crossroads, Directions, and a New Critical Race Theory.* Philadelphia: Temple University Press, 2002.

Vijayan, Prem. "Nationalism and the Developmental State: Exploring Hindutuva Masculinities." *Masculinities Matter! Men, Gender and Development.* Ed. F. Cleaver. London & New York: Zed Books, 2002.

Vitelo, Paul. "A Mayor in the Obama Mold, but Backing Clinton." *The New York Times,* 14 Apr. 2008.

Wallsten, Peter. "Top of the Ticket." 16 Mar. 2008. *Politics Coast to Coast with the LA Times.* Blog. 10 May 2008 <http://latimes blogs.latimes.com/washington/2008/03/throughout-his.html>.

Washington, Ellis. "Du Bois vs. Washington: Old Lessons Black People Have Not Learned." 2001. *Issues and Views*. 12 May 2008 <http://www.issues-views.com/index.php/sect/1000/article/999>.

White, Walter. "A Report from Walter White on the Lynching of Claude Neal." *ChickenBones: A Journal for Literary & Artistic African-American Themes*. 10 May 2008 <http://www.nathaniel turner.com/lynchingclaudeneal.htm>.

Westley, Robert. "Many Billions Gone: Is It Time to Reconsider the Case for Black Reparations?" *Boston College Law Review* XL.1 (Dec. 1998): 429–476.

Williams, Paul, ed. *The International Bill of Human Rights*. Glen Ellen, CA: Entwhistle Books, 1981.

Wilson, William Julius. *The Declining Significance of Race: Blacks and Changing American Institutions*. Chicago: University of Chicago Press, 1980.

Woodward, C. V. *The Strange Career of Jim Crow,* 3rd rev. ed. New York: Oxford University Press, 1974.

INDEX

A

**ADDING SOME
 CONTEXT** 116, v
America, iv
American Negro
 Labor Congress,
 52
Anderson Cooper,
 165
Annie Leibiovitz,
 126
Atlanta Board of
 Education, 37
Atlanta
 Compromise, 32

B

Barack Obama, vii,
 49, 157, 158,
 159, 163, 174,
 177
Bethune, 42, 43
Birth of a Nation,
 14, 112, 127,
 142, 143, 148,
 149, 150, 154,
 178, 179
Black Feminist
 Statement' of
 1977, 46
Black Masculinity
 and the Civil
 Rights Movement
 83, iv
Booker T.
 Washington, 17,
 32, 33, 62
Bootstrapping,
 Victimology, and
 Colorblindness:,
 iv

*Brown v. Board of
 Education*, 3, 56,
 57, 169

C

Cement Boot Straps
 and
 Decontextualizati
 on:, iv
Chief Justice
 Warren, 54
Collective Rights 69,
 iv
**COMMUNISM, RACE-
 BAITING, AND
 BACK-BITING** 24,
 iii
Council on African
 Affairs, 26
Critique of the Class
 Theory 108, iv
Critique Of The
 Neo-Left View
 111, iv

D

diversity pimps, 49
Don Quioxtes, 109
Dred Scott, 1, 104,
 105, 172
Du Bois, 12, 13, 14,
 17, 28, 30, 32,
 33, 34, 35, 37,
 38, 51, 54, 59,
 61, 62, 63, 64,
 65, 67, 69, 120,
 169, 172, 174,
 179, 180

E

Eleanor Roosevelt,
 12, 16, 19, 20,
 21, 22, 23, 37,

38, 39, 40, 41,
 42, 43, 50, 56,
 63, 64, 66, 159,
 171, 173, 178
Elizabeth Minnich,
 45
**EMANCIPATION,
 RECONSTRUCTIO
 N,,** v
**ENVISIONING THE
 REPRESENTATIO
 NAL BLACK MAN**
 147, v
Exporting
 Hegemonic
 Masculinity:
 Actions,, iv

F

Film and Law 120, v
**FILM AS A LEGAL
 LENS** 129, v

G

Garvey, 59, 60, 61,
 62, 173

H

Harold Ford, 111,
 167
HE AIN'T WHITE,
 HE'S MY
 BROTHER 36, iii
hegemonic
 masculinity, 79,
 80, 82, 83, 84,
 86, 87, 98, 103
Hegemonic
 Masculinity, iv,
 83
Hillary Clinton, vii
**HUMAN RIGHTS:
 ANATOMY OF**

ABANDONMENT
9, iii

I

**IN THE BEGINNING
THERE WAS
SLAVERY** 1, iii

J

Jim Crow, ii, vii, 4,
5, 20, 21, 49, 85,
88, 89, 96, 106,
127, 137, 150,
153, 168, 171,
178, 179, 181
John Lewis, 166
John McCain, 167

K

Ku Klux Klan, 14,
60, 61

L

LaNacion, 59
LeBron James, 126
lynchings, 1, 3, 5, 7,
15, 21, 40, 51

M

Marcus Garvey, 59,
60, 61
Martin Luther King,
21, 55, 106, 147
Mary Dudziak, 67
Mary McLeod, 42,
43
Masculinity,
Patriarchy, and
Relationship 82,
iv
Medgar Evers, 21
**MISSISSIPPI
BURNING**, v, 129,
130, 133, 134,
169, 172

Mississippi Burning
123, v
Moorfield Storey, 12

N

NAACP, iii, vi, 1, 3,
4, 7, 11, 12, 13,
14, 16, 17, 18,
19, 20, 21, 23,
24, 26, 27, 28,
32, 33, 34, 35,
37, 38, 39, 40,
41, 42, 43, 50,
51, 52, 53, 54,
55, 56, 57, 59,
61, 62, 63, 64,
65, 67, 68, 69,
73, 76, 102, 103,
120, 139, 170,
176, 177, 178

O

**OF EGOS,
INFIGHTING, AND
THE NAACP** 56,
iii
Ole' Mis' 124, v

P

Paul Robeson, 22, 25
Peggy McIntosh, 43,
47
Performing
Masculinity:
Black, Red,
Brown, and, iv
President Reagan,
111
Professor Derrick
Bell, 57
Professor William
Julius Wilson,
113

R

race, i, ii, vi, vii, 1,
2, 6, 7, 8, 10, 12,
13, 20, 26, 29,
31, 33, 40, 43,
45, 46, 48, 50,
52, 56, 57, 61,
63, 64, 80, 84,
85, 86, 97, 103,
104, 105, 106,
107, 110, 111,
112, 113, 114,
115, 116, 117,
119, 120, 121,
123, 124, 127,
130, 131, 132,
134, 135, 136,
138, 140, 157,
158, 159, 160,
162, 163, 164,
165, 166, 167,
168
**RACE IS A STATE OF
MIND** 98, iv
racism, ii, vi, 4, 8,
16, 25, 29, 32,
39, 40, 43, 44,
46, 48, 49, 56,
67, 80, 85, 88,
100, 102, 105,
106, 107, 108,
109, 110, 112,
113, 114, 115,
116, 117, 118,
119, 120, 130,
132, 133, 134,
135, 138, 151,
157, 158, 163,
165, 166, 168
Rap Music, 98, 174
Roy Wilkins, 26, 39

S

Self-Defining
Identity Politics
and the, v
Services, iv

T

TELEVISION 123, v
THE AMERICAN
  CONSTRUCTION
  OF, iv
The Articulation of
  Race 126, v
THE CIVIL RIGHTS
  MOVEMENT AND
  THE BLACK MAN
  140, v
The Class Theorists:
  It's The Class
  Line,, iv
The Communist
  Party, 53, 177
The CRC, 26
The Crime of
  Government
  Against the
  Negro People' to
  the United
  Nations, 25

The Crisis, 13, 14,
  32, 33, 34, 36,
  51, 59, 61, 172
THE PERFECT
  STORM:
  POLITICS, RACE,
  AND ECONOMICS
  18, iii
The Rap on
  Reparations 94,
  iv
THE RED BADGE OF
  SHAME 48, iii
The UDHR and Its
  Individualistic
  Underpinnings
  66, iv
Tupac Shakur, 98

V

View From the Neo-
  Left 110, iv
Vogue, 126

W

W. E. B. Du Bois, 54
Walter White, 19,
  26, 27, 33, 34,
  35, 36, 37, 38,
  39, 41, 43, 51,
  64, 66, 78, 172,
  173, 180
We Charge
  Genocide, 25, 26,
  177
White Privilege, 47,
  176
William Patterson,
  25

Y

YEZ UM MS.
  ROOSEVELT 39,
  iii

www.ingramcontent.com/pod-product-compliance
Lightning Source LLC
Chambersburg PA
CBHW020354270326
41926CB00007B/430